GRACE

Breakthrough

Bill Giovannetti

G

• Certified First Edition-MaxGrace.com •

BILL GIOVANNETTI

GRACE

Breakthrough

Exploding the Lies
That Wound Your
Confidence and Joy

Endurant Press

ISBN Print edition: 978-0-9836812-5-0

ATTENTION CORPORATIONS, UNIVERSITIES, COLLEGES, CHURCHES and MINISTRY GROUPS: Quantity discounts are available on bulk purchases of this book for educational, gift purposes, group studies, or premiums. Special books or book excerpts can also be created to fit specific needs. Please contact www.maxgrace.com for information.

www.maxgrace.com

CONTENTS

AUTHOR'S NOTE

E'er since by faith I saw the stream
Thy flowing wounds supply,
Redeeming love has been my theme,
And shall be till I die.
-William Cowper, 1700s

I've already written several books on grace, and I have more in the pipeline. You might wonder what makes them different.

- *Grace Intervention* tackles the LEGALISM that hides in the shadows and sucks the grace out of the room.
- *Grace Rehab* peels off the LABELS of doom and defeat slapped on you by the past, and applies the life-affirming new labels given you by God.
- *Grace Breakthrough* (this book) explodes the LIES that wound the confidence and joy that should be yours in Christ.
- *Grace Renovation* (forthcoming) draws the blueprint for a grace-based DISCIPLESHIP plan, so you can build a sustainable spirituality for yourself and your church.

Each one has been a joy to write. I am humbly thankful that God should permit me to pen even one syllable about my Savior's matchless grace.

Bill Giovannetti
Redding, California

INTRO:

BREAKING THROUGH

The ultimate test of our spirituality is the measure of our amazement at the grace of God. – D. Martyn Lloyd-Jones

"But none of these things move me; nor do I count my life dear to myself, so that I may finish my race with joy, and the ministry which I received from the Lord Jesus, to testify to the gospel of the grace of God." (Acts 20:24)

THE MOTHER OF ALL THE DEVIL'S LIES:
"GOD IS LESS THAN HE SAYS HE IS."

IT WAS A DARK AND STORMY NIGHT.

A Wednesday night, to be exact. I had finished teaching a Bible class at my church, and people were filtering out to head home. One newcomer left the building and returned a few minutes later. Raindrops speckled his shoulders and glasses.

"My battery died," he said. "Anybody have cables?"

"Sure," I said. I figured it would be a good way to get to know the new guy. I followed him into the steady drizzle, glad that my jacket had a hood.

I pulled my car next to his, fished out my cables, and handed them over. While he hooked up to his dead battery, I opened my hood. Cold rain splatted our backs and thunder rumbled in the distance. A few dim parking lot lights punctuated the darkness.

Not much chatting happened. We just wanted to be done. New Guy handed me the rain-slickened cables.

Before I attached them, I double-checked: "Red to positive, right?"

"Yes, red to positive."

Seconds later, a sizzle, snap, spark, blinding flash, and near hygienic indiscretion on my end told me one of us was wrong.

I took a deep breath and checked his set-up. He'd attached his cables red to negative.

Yep.

We were reverse polarized.

The Fall

So is the human heart. The Fall—that dark day when the world plunged into sin—reversed our polarities. It inverted our instincts. It wrecked our thoughts about God.

The message of grace crackles and sparks when it touches our innately legalistic spirit.

The Fall made grace feel like a lie, like a big joke on unsuspecting sinners. Too easy. Too good to be true. Too costly to be free.

Grace does not compute.

We might say it does. We might speak of it, sing of it, write of it, and feel goose-bumps over it, but there's little amazement left. On our bad days, the devil has a field-day convincing us that God is less than he says he is. He's less loving, less faithful, less forgiving, and less fatherly.

It's just *grace*—a song lyric, a passing emotion, a spiritual-sounding word to say when we don't know what to say.

It's just a bland niceness on the part of God. A wink and a nod at the bad people. Moral laxity. God, the Heavenly, cookie-dispensing, owie-soothing, hand-patting Grandmother.

Or God the Big Meanie in the sky who grudgingly doles out smidgens of grace on the well-deserving.

In either case, we have made God less than he is, and by so doing, have embraced the mother of all the devil's lies.

We've too often demoted grace to anything but the tough, exacting, profound, complex, interlocking web of ultimate truths that give meaning and depth to our existence. We've squeezed it out of its lofty position as the guiding star of all our thoughts about God.

We've lost the wonder of grace.

How did this happen?

The Lies

It happened because we've swallowed a lie.

The devil is a liar, Jesus said. He's the father of the whole world's lying operation (John 8:44).

Truth is reality. Truth is reality as God experiences it, and God reveals it.

Lies are unreality.

Anything in line with God's reality is truth.

Anything out of line is a falsehood or a lie.

The devil specializes in unreality.

This is a book about the devil's lies, especially his lies against grace.

Because of the Fall, we are natural born suckers for these lies. The Fall put scar tissue over our hearts. It reversed our polarities. It inflicted the human race with the most deadly malady in the world of mankind: Grace Deficit Disorder.

Grace Deficit Disorder leads its sufferers down the pretty little path of joy-killing, self-hating, God-slandering unreality. It infects the soul's operating system. It installs "the doctrines of demons" into the software (1 Timothy 4:1). It blinds the eyes and clouds the mind.

The devil hacks the soul with lies, especially about who God is, and about who you are.

And, because the devil is so subtle, you don't even know its happening. The lies have been installed, and now you've swallowed the ultimate lie, the one that makes God less than he is.

You've embraced the lie that makes grace not grace.

The only way grace gets through is by breaking through.

Grace must explode the lies. It must pierce the scar tissue. It has to punch the devil in the gut and penetrate the dark and stormy night of the soul with the bright light of Calvary Love.

Only this trauma of grace has the power to correct the backwards polarity of the fallen human heart.

Only an encounter with the realities of grace can purge the system of the unrealities of legalism.

A grace breakthrough is the desperate need of every Christian. It is the desperate need of the Church. It is the pressing and urgent need of the world. This recovery of grace—true, deep, scandalous, utterly free grace—is the precursor to revival, and the only hope of a world gone mad.

And, in an irony that has the devil laughing up his crisply-pressed sleeve, it is the one thing our hearts resist most.

Welcome to the journey you need most and want least.

The Spirit's Sword

> For the word of God *is* living and powerful, and sharper than any two-edged sword, piercing even to the division of soul and spirit, and of joints and marrow, and is a discerner of the thoughts and intents of the heart. (Hebrews 4:12)

The Word of God is the Spirit's sword to slice and dice the devil's lies. When you expose yourself to Scripture's truth, the Spirit of God wields his trusty sword to slice through the thickest callous on the hardest heart.

The Word is the tip of your grace breakthrough's spear. It is your ultimate reality check.

Please do not read this book with the thought that you will muscle-up your own grace breakthrough. You'd have an easier time doing cartwheels on the surface of the sun. It requires the supernatural agency of the Holy Spirit coupled with the supernatural instrument of the

Word of God to cut through the legalism that smothers your joy.

Your grace breakthrough is God's work, God's responsibility, and God's burden alone. God's job is to do all the work. Your job is to hear the truth and believe it. Your job is the faith to put yourself in a position to grow deeper in God's grace and truth (2 Peter 3:18). God's job is the breakthrough that happens to you as the result.

At the end of the day, grace makes its own way. Only grace can make grace break through.

God is eager for this. Eager for you. He is the ideal Dad cheering you on.

God is better than you think he is. He's infinitely better than what that old, ugly, beautiful, subtle, lying serpent tells you he is.

It's time to shed your distorted perceptions of God. It's time to exit the land of unreality. It's time to escape to reality. It's time to rest from your labors. It's time to heal the fearsome wounds of Grace Deficit Disorder.

So brew up some coffee—or tea if you're extra fussy—or pour yourself a nice cup of wine. Put your feet up. Open your heart. And expose your mind to nine grace breakthroughs in Scripture. I pray that God will bring you to that golden moment when you're tapped into his still-amazing grace, and you've actually got "red to positive."

Prayer

Gracious Father,

Bring me to a place where your grace so fills my horizon that the devil's death-dealing lies are all crowded out. Teach me to believe that you are who you say you are—that you are immeasurably better to me than I can ask or think. Break through whatever lies I believe about you. Pierce the dark night of my soul with the dawn of Calvary's love. Open my eyes to see never-failing streams of abundant grace all around. And create in me the confidence of a firstborn child of a Great King.

Through Christ, the fountain of all grace, I pray,

Amen.

1

THE GRACE BREAKTHROUGH

But even if our gospel is veiled, it is veiled to those who are perishing, whose minds the god of this age has blinded, who do not believe, lest the light of the gospel of the glory of Christ, who is the image of God, should shine on them. (2 Corinthians 4:3,4)

Amazing grace! How sweet the sound, / That saved a wretch like me! / I once was lost but now am found, / Was blind but now I see. –John Newton, 1700s

BIG LIE #1: I'VE GOT GRACE ALL FIGURED OUT.

IT'S JUST A WORD... GRACE. **A simple word. A common word.** Everybody says it. Every religion claims it. The most widely sung lyric in all the world exalts it: *Amazing Grace.*

The Bible says,

> For you know the grace of our Lord Jesus Christ, that though He was rich, yet for your sakes He became poor, that you through His poverty might become rich. (2 Corinthians 8:9)

If you know Christ, you are, by definition, rich. This verse says so. Which leads to what might be the most common problem among Christians today: Most of God's children limp beneath their true riches in grace.

Grace makes every child of God rich in blessings money can't buy.

It's time to start believing that. It's time to start *feeling* that too.

Grace theology needs to become grace psychology. That's one of Scripture's big ideas. More than a doctrine. More than mental assent. More than a passing emotion. Grace can become a deeply-rooted, Scripture-based, trouble-hardened instinctive way of taking on every day by the power and love of God.

What's in a Word?

A word is a place-holder for an idea.

I'm from Chicago, the pizza capital of the galaxy.

If I say the word *pizza*, certain ideas come into your mind. Certain images. Certain smells and tastes and memories. Those ideas fire off a memo to your salivary glands, and soon you're drooling. I would bet that what comes into my mind with the word pizza is a whole lot different than what comes into your mind.

An old time pastor named A.W. Tozer once said, "What comes into your mind when you hear the word *God* is the most important thing about you."

He was saying that a word is a place-holder for an idea, a reality, a truth, a concept, a person. He was saying your thoughts about God define you.

Tozer was right.

I would add that, "What comes into your mind when you hear the word *grace* is the second most important thing about you."

I'm on a mission to help make sure that what comes into people's minds when they hear the word grace is supremely biblical and utterly exalted.

I pray that your idea of grace matches the Bible's idea of grace. God's idea of grace. The exact meaning of the word *grace* should be crystal clear to every child of God.

Let's launch an awakening around the country and around the world in our generation.

It's time to explode the lies that wound your confidence and kill your joy. The lie that you've got grace all figured out.

It's time to shake off the shackles of other people's rules.

It's time to break free from dark forces that hold your life in depression, discouragement, disillusionment, guilt, shame, and defeat.

It's time to smash into a gooey mess the forces that stink up our testimony and make unbelieving friends completely disinterested in our gospel.

And it's time for you and me and all of us to step into the sunny highlands of the glittering, glorious grace of Almighty God.

You are ready for this.

Grace Breakthrough

I've used the word *breakthrough* on purpose. Our inbred legalism calls for nothing less than a traumatic encounter with a force beyond our understanding. Only a breakthrough can challenge a person's status quo.

Legalism is the ultimate blind spot, and it wrecks our joy and our walk with God.

Nobody in the Bible ever understood grace without a breakthrough. They needed a smack upside the head, or a kick in the seat of the pants.

Grace is traumatic. Grace is a crisis. It's a total reversal of everything you thought you knew about about God.

It's the opposite of everything you're sure about.

There's a simple reason why we all need a Grace Breakthrough: *The unrenewed heart is terminally infected with a built-in resistance to the grace of God.*

We're naturally blind to it. Hardened against it.

> ...[H]aving their understanding darkened, being alienated from the life of God, because of the ignorance that is in them, because of the blindness [callous] of their heart. (Ephesians 4:18)

By nature, people are blind to grace. There's a grace-blackout in the soul.

My wife, Margi was talking with an old friend a little while ago. He said, "I'm reading one of Bill's books on legalism and grace, but it really doesn't apply to me." He said, "I didn't come from a legalistic background, and so that stuff isn't really for me."

Margi laughed when she told me about it. She said, "This is the same man who interrupted his daughter's wedding reception to give a speech about the evils of dancing and drinking. Shaming was his spiritual gift."

This is the same man whose grown kids abandoned Christianity because they couldn't stand the rules. They couldn't stand the judgmentalism and narrowness they grew up with.

So they gave up on God.

"Legalism and grace isn't my problem," this self-deluded man said.

In the Bible, no Pharisee ever thought being a Pharisee was a problem. People are blind to their own legalism.

It's possible you're reading this and thinking: "What an out-of-touch legalist! I am so glad I am not at all like him, not even one little bit."

That is exactly what makes teaching on grace so difficult. You may not interrupt weddings with denunciations of the evils of dancing, but do you routinely doubt the love of God?

Do you think you've got grace all figured out because you enjoy microbrews and sport the latest socially approved facial hair, tats, and piercings? Great. But if you're defeated emotionally by dysfunctions Christ has defeated spiritually, you need a breakthrough.

Do you think you're better than other people in God's eyes? Worse than other people?

Do you resent God's grace in their lives?

Do ever feel that God owes you? The world owes you? Anybody owes you?

Does serving God wear you out?

Legalists are blind to their own legalism. Jesus called them "Blind guides, who strain out a gnat and swallow a camel" (Matthew 23:24).

The first breakthrough you need is breaking through your blindness to grace. You need to confess you don't have grace all figured out. We all need to tell God, "I need this thing called grace more than I ever realized."

Your own self-made success might be your biggest enemy in this. Just because you're successful in finance or family, bodybuilding or social media, it doesn't mean you're a success with God. That's the hard lesson the Pharisees never learned.

So they stayed in their little fairy-land where grace was optional. Or only for emergencies. Or only on occasion when the really bad secrets of their lives reared their heads.

Let's allow for the possibility that we're not as grace-oriented as we think we are. Let's grant that we might have some legalistic blinders on, some corners of the heart still festering with the pus and pain of Grace Deficit Disorder.

I'd like to outline seven spiritual symptoms of Grace Deficit Disorder. Add up how many apply to you, because the higher your number, the more infected you are. And the more you need to allow for the fact that you're swamped by legalism and might not even know it.

Seven People Who Desperately Need A Grace Breakthrough

1. Whiny People

If you are basically a whiny person, you need a Grace Breakthrough. The reason is simple: *you are emotionally out of touch with your blessings as a child of God.*

For a case study, consider the children of God wandering in the wilderness:

> And the people spoke against God and against Moses: "Why have you brought us up out of Egypt to die in the wilderness? For there is no food and no water, and our soul loathes this worthless bread." (Numbers 21:5)

When I was an Awana leader (a church-based kids' club), I took a bunch of kids to the top of the tallest building in the world at that time, in Chicago. Back in the day, it was called the Sears Tower. The views are awesome. You can see Soldier Field where the Bears play football. You can see Lake Michigan and its shoreline. All the skyscrapers, and highways radiating out to the suburbs. You could see Chicago stretching out forever.

One little kid came to me and asked, "So, where's Chicago?"

"Where's Chicago?" I said. "It's everywhere you look!"

Scripture tells the story of God's people on the way to the Promised Land. For forty years, God made sure their shoes didn't wear out. God protected them in every battle. God provided water every time they ran out.

Plus, God fed them by a miracle every single day — a bread called *manna*. It grew on the ground, and the people ate it every day. It was delicious. The Bible calls it, "the food of angels" (Psalm 78:25).

God's blessing was everywhere they looked, just like it is for you.

And yet, here they were, whining again.

You brought us here to die.

You don't care about us.

And get this... "our *souls* loathe this worthless bread."

It wasn't a taste problem; it was a soul problem.

"Where's the grace?" they whined.

Where's the grace? It was everywhere they looked.

If you find yourself routinely whining about your life and your world, you need a grace breakthrough. You are emotionally out of touch with the fountain of blessings flowing down to you from heaven every single minute.

Are you a whiny person? Score one if you are. Keep count.

2. Anxious People

If you are a basically an anxious person, you also need a grace breakthrough.

By anxious, I mean that worries and fears actually dominate your life and hurt your relationships. Everybody has fears and worries as part of the normal emotions of life. These are the everyday concerns that are part of being human, and that's not what I'm talking about. There are also some people who have a medical condition that makes them anxious — I'm not talking about you either, and that applies to all these profiles we'll cover.

I am talking about being dominated by worries and fears because of unresolved trials from your past.

Anxious people need a grace breakthrough, and the reason is simple: *you are out of touch emotionally with the protecting hand of God.*

Grace Deficit Disorder means that your emotions have not yet caught up to your theology.

For our case study, let's look at the disciples. Jesus told them to get on a boat, and then a huge storm blew in. They started bailing, and they freaked out. A few minutes into this, they notice that Jesus is missing. Where is he?

> But He was in the stern, asleep on a pillow. And they awoke Him and said to Him, "Teacher, do You not care that we are perishing?" Then He arose and rebuked the wind, and said to the sea, "Peace, be still!" And the wind ceased and there was a great calm. But He said to them, "Why are you so fearful [intimidated]? How is it that you have no faith?" (Mark 4:38-40)

Grace requires tough love. Jesus did not say, "Oh, you poor little bunnies! That had to be so scary! I am very sorry that happened to you."

Nope.

What did he do?

He rebuked them. *Toughen up! Why are you so wimpy?* You could make the case that the Greek word translated "fearful" actually means "wimpy."

Jesus expected better from them. After all, they had seen him do miracles already. Now they found him sleeping through the storm. That fact should have told them something. As long as he was with them, grace was with them, and that should have been enough.

> Be anxious for nothing, but in everything by prayer and supplication, with thanksgiving, let your requests be made known to God; and the peace of God, which surpasses all understanding, will guard your hearts and minds through Christ Jesus. (Philippians 4:6, 7)

That is the same lesson God is teaching you. Anxious people need a breakthrough too.

3. Judgmental People

If you are basically a critical, judgmental person, you need a grace breakthrough.

That's because you are emotionally out of touch with the depths of your own forgiveness before God.

Jesus told this parable about a king who had a servant who owed him money. The servant couldn't pay up, so the king ordered that the servant's family be sold to pay the bills.

The servant fell down and pled for mercy. The king was moved with compassion, and he forgave the debt.

Nice story, right?

Just like God has forgiven you, because of the Cross of Christ, and the blood Jesus shed there. Total forgiveness for all your moral debts, past, present, and future.

It's a wonderful story.

But then the story Jesus told turns not so nice.

> But that servant went out and found one of his fellow servants who owed him a hundred denarii; and he laid hands on him and took him by the throat, saying, "Pay me what you owe!" So his fellow servant fell down at his feet and begged him, saying, "Have patience with me, and I will pay you all." And he would not, but went and threw him into prison till he should pay the debt. (Matthew 18:28-30)

Do you see the disconnect here? How many times have you appointed yourself as critic, corrector, judge, and jury? How many times have you looked down your pointy nose at people who messed up? How many times have you looked at sinners, and said, "I am so glad that I'm not as horrible as you!"?

You have forgotten the hole you were in. You have lost sight of the grace God extended to you.

Before he was saved, Paul hated Christians with a passion and judged them mercilessly. Then he had his grace breakthrough, and God knocked him silly and blind and right off his horse. After that, this critic of others would stand and say, *I am the chief of sinners...* He followed that up with, *I am what I am by the grace of God.*

Judgmental people stand radically in need of a grace breakthrough. Are you keeping track?

4. Insecure People

If you are basically an insecure person, and you don't like yourself, and can't accept yourself just as you are, you also need a grace breakthrough.

That is because you are emotionally out of touch with God's radically profound acceptance of you in Christ. You doubt his infinite ability to use you in mighty ways for his purposes, just as you are.

God told Moses to go to Egypt, and set his people free.

Moses said, "Who am I? I'm sure this is a big mistake, and you've got the wrong person."

God said, "Don't worry about who you are, instead rest in who I am."

Moses said, "They won't believe me."

God said, "I'll make them believe you."

Moses said,

O my Lord, I am not eloquent, neither before nor
since You have spoken to Your servant; but I am slow
of speech and slow of tongue. (Exodus 4:10)

God said, "Now therefore, go, and I will be with your
mouth and teach you what you shall say" (Exodus 4:12).

Chronic insecurity (non-medical) is a sure symptom
of Grace Deficit Disorder.

I have to raise my hand here and testify. Much of
what I do, I feel insecure about. Will people like me?
Will I be successful? Can I hide my shortcomings? Can I
get through another sermon, another book, or another
college class without making a fool of myself?

So here's the big breakthrough that I've been making:
Legalism isn't just living by strict rules and regulations,
and being superior and hypocritical and all that —
though all that expresses legalism. Legalism is
something deeper.

You can have a great *theology* of grace, yet still be
dominated by your insecurities, your anxieties, and your
fears.

A person can be theologically educated and
emotionally wrecked.

To whatever degree grace theology has not healed
your broken psychology — your insecurities and fears,
your grandiosity, your immaturity, your entitlement,
your laziness, your bitterness, your vengefulness — to
whatever degree your grace theology has not healed
your broken psychology, your striving for God will be
legalism.

God doesn't want that striving.

He wants you to be made whole first. And you can be made whole. Grace isn't just an academic concept; it's a whole new operating system in your mind, will, and emotions.

When Paul got saved, he hunkered down in an out-of-the way place for three years before he began his public ministry.

Why? He had a whole lot of dysfunctions to heal. He had a huge new operating system to install.

Legalism creates a life motivated more by the deficits in your emotions than by the gratitude in your heart for your blood-bought salvation. It makes you insecure—or hyper-secure in ways that mask your insecurities. You need a breakthrough.

5. Guilty People

If your life is dominated by guilt and shame, you need a breakthrough too.

That's because the devil keeps accusing you, and you don't have answers for him yet. *You are emotionally out of touch with the all-sufficiency of Christ's death on the Cross.*

The Cross is the answer to all your guilt and shame. There, on that gnarly hill called Calvary, stands the answer to all your self-punishing psychosis. There, in Christ's shed blood — there in the truths the Bible labels *redemption, propitiation, justification,* and *regeneration,* you will find deliverance from guilt and shame.

When the prodigal son came home, he expected to grovel before his father.

His father wouldn't let him. Instead, the father convened a grace breakthrough in the form of a party, complete with dancing and prime beef on the spit.

This son was a horrible person. He did unspeakable things. He deserved judgment. He got grace.

That is the beauty of the gospel.

And that same gospel is yours. That immense outpouring of divine grace. Nothing washes away the guilt and shame of a lifetime like the flood of Calvary's love. Dive deeply into that flood. Feel its cleansing power.

You can stop beating yourself up. You can quit taking it out on other people. You can end your lifetime of penance. If you really get this, it will make you humble, not cocky.

Whatever guilt your sins deserved, Jesus took onto himself at the Cross. Whatever shame, whatever punishment, whatever condemnation, whatever death—every consequence your sins merited were paid in full by Christ on the day he shed his blood.

To grovel in guilt and shame is to under-value the Cross of Christ. It is a sure sign you need a grace breakthrough.

6. *Overwhelmed People*

Yes, overwhelmed people. And I mean overwhelmed as a way of life. There will always be overwhelming *seasons* of life for all of us. That is normal, and that is not what I mean.

Here, I mean that you have made yourself chronically too busy to breathe.

That's because you are emotionally motivated to prove something, or to punish yourself, or to, in some sad way, perform your way into a sense of acceptance and worth.

My case study here is Martha. Jesus came for dinner to the home of Martha and her sister, Mary. Mary visited with Jesus in the living room. Martha cooked dinner in the kitchen. Being Italian, I know where I would be.

Finally, she cracked:

> But Martha was distracted with much serving, and she approached Him and said, "Lord, do You not care that my sister has left me to serve alone? Therefore tell her to help me." And Jesus answered and said to her, "Martha, Martha, you are worried and troubled about many things. But one thing is needed, and Mary has chosen that good part, which will not be taken away from her." (Luke 10:40-42)

Like a good legalist, she takes it out on Jesus.

All I can say is this: if you're so busy you can't breathe or put margin in your life, you're trying to solve an emotional hole that only grace can fill.

You need a breakthrough.

Okay, so there are six profiles of grace-deficient people, and there's only one left.

Did I get you yet? Are you included?

No?

Okay. I don't want you to feel left out, so here's one more certain sign you desperately need a grace breakthrough.

7. Smug People

Smug people need a breakthrough.

That is because they are emotionally out of touch with their desperate need for grace. Self-satisfied self-effort can never please our self-sufficient God.

You need grace more than you realize.

For a case study, let's turn to the religious leaders of the Jews. Israel had been conquered by the Roman Empire. A Roman governor ruled over them, and the flag of Rome flew above Jerusalem.

Jesus told them, "You shall know the truth, and the truth shall make you free" (John 8:32).

The leaders got indignant. What do you mean *free?* We're already free! We're exalted children of Father Abraham!

Jesus probably didn't know whether to laugh or cry. They called themselves free, but what about that Roman flag flying over there? They were under the thumb of the Roman government, paying crazy-high taxes to Caesar, and anything but free.

And what about the rivers of blood flowing down from their temple? Endless requirements for endless sacrifices. A thousand picky rules for every detail of life, even down to how they washed their hands. A life of duty and obligation with no assurance of salvation. They were slaves to their own religious traditions, yet they called themselves free.

And what about their sins? What about their offenses against the blazing holiness of an all-consuming God? They were trapped in guilt and shame, in addiction and defeat, yet they called themselves free.

"We are children of Abraham! We have never been slaves to anybody!" How did Jesus not laugh in their faces?

Smug people.

The unrenewed heart is trapped in terminal denial. Swarmed by the devil's lies. The first grace breakthrough requires breaking through the blindness to your own need of a grace breakthrough.

So what's your score?

Actually, it doesn't really matter. Anybody who thinks they have grace all figured out—yet lives in uncertainty, fear, arrogance, or any other dysfunction—still has some growing to do. They've swallowed a lie. They've shrunken God's grace.

An infinite panorama of divine love stretches out before us; let's explore every square inch if it.

Whoever you are, however long you may have walked with God, can't you sink deeper roots into his grace? Isn't there yet more room for you to grow in grace? Aren't there still corners of your mind yet unrenewed by the matchless mercies of God (Romans 12:2)?

What comes to your mind when you hear the word grace?

If you are breathing, you need a grace breakthrough, and that is what we will explore in these pages.

Let the sparks fly.

Prayer

O Lord,

Please pull off my blinders. Awaken my heart to your love. Deliver me from the lie that I've got grace all figured out. Show me oceans of love I have yet to explore.

Where I am whiny, make me thankful. Where I am anxious, make me brave. Where I am judgmental, make me compassionate and full of merciful love. Strengthen me in my insecurities. Deliver me from guilt and shame. When the floods of life overwhelm me, be my rock and hold me tightly. Find whatever spirit of smugness I may show, Lord humble me that I might experience the grace that's always there.

Lord Jesus, live through me.

I pray in your name alone,

Amen.

2

The Gospel Breakthrough

And you too trusted him, when you had heard the message of truth, the gospel of your salvation. And after you gave your confidence to him you were, so to speak, stamped with the promised Holy Spirit as a pledge of our inheritance, until the day when God completes the redemption of what is his own; and that will again be to the praise of his glory. (Ephesians 1:13, 14, Phil)

Let this be to you the mark of true Gospel preaching - where Christ is everything, and the creature is nothing; where it is salvation all of grace, through the work of the Holy Spirit applying to the soul the precious blood of Jesus. -Charles Spurgeon, 1800s

Big Lie #2: God will commit himself to me when I commit myself to him with enough determination.

WHEN I BEGAN AS A young pastor, there were several mentors in my life. One of them was an ancient pastor named Lance B. Latham. Everybody called him Doc.

Doc was the guy who started what is now the world-wide Awana Youth Association, to help kids learn God's Word. He was eighty-ish when I started working as a pastor at the church he founded. He looked like he was three-hundred.

I shared many conversations with him, but there's one that rises head and shoulders above the rest for the impact it had on me.

We were in the old basement of our church in Chicago. Hard tiled floors made our voices echo, and the place was drafty and cold. A little Copy Room was tucked beneath a concrete stairway — wooden shelves overflowing with reams of paper, and an old mimeograph machine on a large wooden bench. I can still smell that ink.

I don't remember why we were both in that cramped Copy Room, but I do remember asking Doc a question.

I said, "Doc, I know so many people who say they believe in Jesus, but I know they're not saved. They don't understand the gospel. They think baptism or communion or good works will get them to heaven. They believe these lies. But they still say they believe in Jesus. Doc, I don't get it."

Tall, and slender, with pure white hair, Doc aimed sparkling blue eyes at me and said one sentence that stuck with me all these years.

He said, "Bill, where is their hope for eternity?"

I don't remember the rest of our conversation, but I remember that question.

Where is their hope for eternity?

What are they counting on for eternal life? Where have they turned for forgiveness of sins, for peace with God, and for entrance to heaven? What is their ground, their basis, their reason why God should make them his own?

Where is their hope for eternity?

That little question triggered a breakthrough for me. The lights came on. They've never turned off. The gospel of grace sparkled for me like a million diamonds, and it has never lost its luster.

It's time to think through the mother of all breakthroughs: the Gospel Breakthrough.

Five Indispensable Facts about the Gospel

1. Its Definition

The gospel describes the world's only hope in all its Ultra-High-Definition glory.

The gospel is the entry way into the family and plan of God. If life with God is a mansion, the gospel is the doorway into the mansion. Unless you have crossed the gospel threshold, you are still outside.

Think of it this way. In the Bible, there are thousands of truths. Tens of thousands. Promises. Doctrines. Commands. Ideas. Stories.

There's a whole lot of truths in these Bibles of ours. But salvation doesn't require us to know them all, thankfully. There's a subset, a data-pack, an information download that comprises the gospel.

> How then shall they call on Him in whom they have not believed? And how shall they believe in Him of whom they have not heard? And how shall they hear without a preacher? (Romans 10:14)

The gospel is a hearable, tellable subset of all biblical truths. Simply put, *the gospel is the irreducible minimum of specific truths a person must hear and respond to in order to be saved.*

Defining that subset actually isn't as tricky as it might sound.

2. Its Nature

By nature, the gospel is good news. That's what the word Gospel means.

That means that when a person first hears the gospel, it feels too good to be true.

Have you ever felt that way about what Jesus offers you? That it sounds too good to be true? If not, maybe you've never actually heard the good news of God's commitment to you, unpolluted by the misconception that you must commit yourself to him in order to be saved.

The gospel is good news because it offers a free gift.

It is good news because it wipes human sweat off the table.

It is good news because it is paid in full by Christ.

It is good news because it requires zero performance, zero improvement, zero obligation, zero duty, and zero worthiness.

It is good news because it permanently decouples your moral performance from God's grace and love to you. The gospel explodes the lie that if you are good to God, he will be good to you. No. God loves you because of who and what he is, never because of who and what you are.

So the gospel defined is this: "The gospel is the irreducible minimum of truths a person must hear and respond to in order to be saved."

And the nature of this subset of truth is that it is always and forever good news.

But we still haven't specified the subset; let's do that now.

3. Its Core

At the core of the gospel stands the Savior, crucified and risen again. If Jesus Christ's death on the Cross is not mentioned and explained at least a little bit, then the gospel is not being communicated.

Scripture reveals the heart of God. So what do we see there?

The heart of Scripture is Christ.

The heart of Christ is grace.

The heart of Grace is the Cross.

That agonizing death of our Savior on Calvary's cross shows forth the heart of the heart of the heart of God.

> Moreover, brethren, I declare to you the gospel which I preached to you, which also you received and in which you stand, by which also you are saved, if you hold fast that word which I preached to you—unless you believed in vain. For I delivered to you first of all that which I also received: that Christ died for our sins according to the Scriptures... (1 Corinthians 15:1-3)

Here is the gospel, Paul says. He sums it up in five little words: *Christ died for our sins.* Five monosyllables. Any child can pronounce them.

Christ died... that part is history. If you had been there, you would have seen it.

For our sins... that part is theology. That part you need to have explained to you, taught to you, illuminated to you. You wouldn't have seen it with your physical eyes; it was a spiritual reality that God had to reveal.

Add together this bit of history with this bit of theology, and you have the gospel.

What it means is that whatever had to happen to pay for your sins happened the day Christ died.

When he died, your sins were punished and judged and erased and paid for and condemned. This hulking force of evil, this sewer of sin which alienated you from God and barred you from heaven and broke your spirit—this is what Christ dealt with for you on the Cross.

Because he was condemned, there is no condemnation for you.

Because he died, you don't have to.

That is the indispensable core, the irreducible minimum. To speak the gospel is to speak of Christ's cross. No Cross, no gospel. It's the heart of the heart of the heart of God's good news.

4. Its Response

The response to the gospel is faith. The gospel summons all people everywhere to believe on the Lord Jesus Christ.

> In Him you also trusted, after you heard the word of truth, the gospel of your salvation; in whom also,

having believed, you were sealed with the Holy Spirit
of promise. (Ephesians 1:13)

You trusted. You believed. These are the same thing.
Synonyms.

What does it mean?

It means you rested your faith in Jesus Christ as your
only hope for salvation, for time, and for eternity.

Your hope to be forgiven.

Your hope to be set free.

Your hope to be adopted into God's forever family.

Do you realize what this means? The fact that God
requires faith alone explodes the lie that makes
salvation some kind of trade between you and God.
"God, I'll give you thirty years of service and
commitment if you forgive all my sins."

No. It's not your commitment at all. God doesn't wait
for you to commit yourself to him before he commits
himself to you. He knows he'd be waiting a very, very
long time for that to happen.

It's not commitment, it's faith. It's trusting Jesus and
his Cross.

You trusted in Christ, believing on him as your only
hope. In that first nano-second, you were sealed into the
family of God.

You stepped out of the howling storms of legalism
and shame and sin and dysfunction and guilt. You
stepped across the threshold into the warmth of life
eternal, and the Holy Spirit slammed the door shut
behind you.

You are sealed into this grace by the "Holy Spirit of
promise" (Ephesians 1:13).

One day you will stand, before the high court of heaven. God the judge will speak. "Give me one good reason," he will say. "Point to one good reason why I should let you into heaven."

Where will you point? To your own good deeds? Your good works? Your religious commitment? Your obedience? Your morality? Where will you point?

I know where I'm pointing: I will point to Jesus Christ, and I will say, "He's all my reason and my only reason, and if Jesus is not enough, I've got no Plan B."

> My faith has found a resting place,
> Not in device or creed;
> I trust the ever-living One,
> His wounds for me shall plead.
>
> I need no other argument,
> I need no other plea,
> It is enough that Jesus died,
> And that He died for me.
> (Eliza E. Hewitt, 1891)

The response to the gospel is faith alone in Christ alone.

By now you're thinking, Bill, let's cover something radical. Something scandalous. I want to make a breakthrough.

Okay. Here we go.

5. *Its Distortions*

We humans are hopelessly addicted to tinkering with God's perfect gospel formula. It's like adding brush strokes to the Mona Lisa. Or adding lines to the *Hallelujah Chorus*. Or putting ketchup on my grandma's lasagna.

The gospel is perfect. Don't mess with perfection.

> But even if we, or an angel from heaven, preach any other gospel to you than what we have preached to you, let him be accursed (Galatians 1:8).

I cannot tell you how many clichés Christians have invented that flip over the good news of God's commitment to you into the bad news of your commitment to God.

Let's explode those lies.

Distortion 1:
"Give Your Life to Christ"

Consider: Who exactly is the giver and who is the receiver in the equation of salvation?

Salvation does not consist of what you give to Christ but of what he gave to you. He gave his life for you that he might put his life into you.

Ditto for "give him your everything." "Give him your all." And all that other stuff in which you're the giver. You've got nothing to give. Nothing to perform. Nothing to do.

Aren't you a bankrupt sinner? Don't your good deeds add up to a pile of filthy rags (Isaiah 64:6)? Aren't you dead in trespasses and sins? Dead?

How can you give something you don't even have? You don't have a life to give to God. You're dead.

Yet it falls so readily off the lips: "She gave her life to Christ," people say. Everybody cheers.

And I have no doubts that she was saved, because God is not that picky when it comes to how we express our faith to him.

But it's our job to keep the gospel straight. To not muddy the streams of grace. Instructing anybody to give anything to God for their salvation makes grace no longer grace.

Distortion 2:
"Follow Christ"

Following Christ isn't the means of salvation; it's the means of sanctification (what comes *after* salvation). It isn't how you get saved; it's how you live saved. The gospel's threshold is never, "Hey Sinner, change your life." It's always, "Hey Sinner, change the object of your faith... and believe on the Lord Jesus Christ."

I talked to a young preacher who made the statement, "I don't invite people to be saved, I invite people to follow Christ. It's a journey with Jesus." He looked proud of his position.

So I said, "How can they go on a journey if they are dead in trespasses and sins? They can't walk."

The gospel of "following Jesus" sets salvation on a shelf so high it's impossibly out of reach.

Following Christ is works-salvation. Following Christ for salvation is legalism. Following Christ — for a person who's locked in sin and shame — is impossible.

The good news is always the effortless "unwork" of trusting Someone Else and His work: "Believe on the Lord Jesus Christ and you will be saved."

When a preacher tells lost people to follow Christ, what they *hear* is a lifetime of duty and obligation. No matter how many qualifiers the preacher adds on, and no matter how much the preacher promises God's grace will do it, it makes no difference. Salvation by the sweat of the brow can never mesh with salvation by the blood of the Cross.

Following is imitating.

And the imitation of Christ never saved a single soul.

I do not want to create a legalism of language where we go around judging people because they don't say the gospel the exact way we want them to. That would be ungracious. Even more, God saves all people who come to Christ no matter what words the evangelist uses.

Still, let's keep the good news good.

If you really must have "following" then here you go:

> Surely goodness and mercy shall follow me / All the days of my life; / And I will dwell in the house of the LORD Forever. (Psalm 23:6)

Distortion 3:
"Ask Jesus Into Your Heart"

Ask Jesus into your heart. Please quit saying this. It's not in the Bible. It doesn't call a person to *exclusive* faith in Christ — meaning you can ask Jesus into your heart, and still be counting on your good works or other stuff for your salvation.

Plus, it paints the wrong picture. Kids picture a literal mini-"G.I. Jesus" inside the organ that pumps their blood.

Worst of all, it bypasses the Cross altogether. It diverts attention from the Old Rugged Cross to the Dirty Old Heart.

Yes, having Jesus within you is the *consequence* of salvation. When you believe in Jesus, he moves inside you. He indwells you forever. You now have, "Christ in you, the hope of glory" (Colossians 1:27).

Even so, you can "ask Jesus into your heart" and still believe in a works salvation. You can "ask him into your heart" and still worship other gods.

You can ask him into your heart and have no clue about what those words even mean.

It's a cliché that needs to go away.

Distortion 4:
"Count the Cost"

Count the cost. Okay, let's do that. Let's calculate the cost of our salvation: 3 nails, plus 1 cross, plus 2 hands, plus 2 feet, plus 1 broken body = 1 life poured out for your eternal salvation.

There and there alone is the cost, and it was paid in full by somebody other than you.

But what about "cheap grace"?

That torpedo has been fired at a pure-grace gospel for far too long. Let's break it down.

Cheap can mean *free*, in which case it is a fine, though redundant, modifier of grace. But cheap can also mean *of poor quality*, in which case it suggests that a free cross-centered grace is a substandard grace.

That is the charge: that by lowering the threshold for salvation, by holding back requirements for a changed life till *after* a person is saved, we have created a costless, and therefore, substandard, grace. They say it's meaningless, and it doesn't save. A cheap, lousy, substandard version of grace.

All of this is legalism's finest hour. It is a pious pile of steaming manure (check out Philippians 3:8, KJV).

The only way to cheapen grace is to propose a price humans can actually afford to pay. Any gospel that requires a price other than the blood of Christ, by definition, cheapens grace. If the death of Christ on Calvary's Cross did not purchase a grace of the highest standard, then what did it purchase? And how can any coin we might add—be it commitment, surrender, dedication, following Christ, or "life-change"—how can anything we add to his purchase price actually make it of greater value? Wouldn't even a molecule of our sweat cheapen the whole thing?

No. It's the legalists who cheapen grace. It's those who preach a high-demand, human-centered, works-requiring false gospel.

If the gospel you hear isn't all of Christ and all of grace, it is no gospel at all. It is, instead, the bad news of the devil's lie wrapped in Christianized lingo.

Spit it out.

Distortion 5:
"Make Jesus Your Lord and Master"

I've been saved for decades, and I'm still working on this one. No, we're not stepping off on the first leg of heresy. Jesus is Lord. He is, was, and always will be Master and Commander of the Universe. He is God above all and deserving of our obedience, and honor, and praise. That will never change.

To say he is Lord is to say he is God, and as God he remains forever the one and only Savior.

People can be saved while being somewhat confused about his person, nature, and work. We all have our growing to do.

But people cannot be saved while positively denying his person, nature, and work. They must come to Jesus as the God of their salvation. That's what this verse is saying:

> Therefore I make known to you that no one speaking by the Spirit of God calls Jesus accursed, and no one can say that Jesus is Lord except by the Holy Spirit. (1 Corinthians 12:3)

Yes, Jesus is Lord.

But responding to him as Lord is utterly impossible for an unsaved person still trapped in sins. To impose the Lordship of Christ on an unsaved person is to preach salvation by works. You cannot serve him as your master until he has transformed you as your Savior. And once you have received him as your Savior by simple, naked, costless faith, then and only then can you begin to grow in following him as Lord. To preach

"Make Jesus your Lord and Master" is to preach a works salvation.

The Scandal of Grace

All of these distortions have one common quality: they cast the weight of salvation on the sinner's stooped shoulders. They make it more about your commitment to God than about his commitment to you.

That's the devil's favorite lie.

Let's explode it.

Here is the scandal of grace. If you never did one good thing for God, he would still take you to heaven, on the power of the shed blood of Christ applied to the doorposts of your soul.

If you are ticked off that I just wrote that, you've believed the lie.

We have the perfect gospel. Don't touch it. Just deliver it, and let God do the rest. It's that simple.

They say, be radical for Jesus. The gospel says, Jesus was radical for you.

They say, commit your life to Christ. The gospel says, Christ committed his life to you.

They say, show crazy love for Jesus. The gospel says, Christ showed crazy love to you.

They say, be All In for Jesus. The gospel says, Christ is all in for you.

They say, be a fanatic for Jesus. The gospel says, Christ was a fanatic for you.

They say, Follow Jesus. The gospel says, Jesus followed you with mercy and grace till he caught you in his loving arms.

It's not you

It's not you, by obedience.

It's not you, by works.

It's not you, by performance.

It's not you, by morality.

It's not you, by religion.

It's not you, by goodness.

It's not you, by any effort, duty, obligation, blood, sweat, or tears.

It's just not you.

The gospel is Christ.

Christ alone.

No surer test can be applied to any truth claiming to be the gospel than this: *What does it make of Christ Jesus and him crucified?* Is he part of it, or is he all?

Where is your hope for eternity?

There was a day, long ago, when a little Italian boy sat on an overstuffed sofa in a Sunday School class in Chicago. And that little boy somehow rested his faith in a Savior who died for him and rose again.

On that day God proved true.

He'll prove true for you, too. Where is your hope for eternity?

Prayer

Gracious Lord,

How I thank you for this beautiful gospel of grace. Pure grace, nothing but grace. I worship you, Lord Jesus, for your death on Calvary's Cross. There, you washed my sins away. There, you shattered the barrier that kept me from God. Whatever punishment, condemnation, guilt, and shame my sins deserved, you accomplished there. When you cried, "It is finished," you cemented this gospel of grace in place for all the ages long.

I bless you for the Cross. And I thank you that you did not place salvation out of reach of the humblest person who believes. Faith alone in Christ alone.

What a gospel! And what a Savior!

Lord Jesus, I confess you as my only hope for life, for eternity, for forgiveness, and for adoption into your family. I am so grateful for the people who first shared your good news with me.

I pray that others will find the same treasure that I found when you found me.

In Christ's grace,

Amen.

3

THE SECURITY BREAKTHROUGH

"And I give them eternal life, and they shall never perish; neither shall anyone snatch them out of My hand. My Father, who has given *them* to Me, is greater than all; and no one is able to snatch *them* out of My Father's hand. (John 10:28, 29)

If one dear saint of God had perished, so might all; if one of the covenant ones be lost, so may all be; and then there is no gospel promise true, but the Bible is a lie, and there is nothing in it worth my acceptance. I will be an infidel at once when I can believe that a saint of God can ever fall finally. If God hath loved me once, then He will love me forever. -C.H. Spurgeon, 1800s

BIG LIE #3: IF I DON'T STAY FAITHFUL TO GOD, HE WON'T STAY FAITHFUL TO ME.

EVERYBODY SINGS ABOUT Amazing Grace, but very few Christians really understand what it means. What is grace? And what difference does it make?

In its simplest form, grace is God doing good things for people who only deserve bad things.

Under grace, God doesn't do these good things because he is nice.

He does these good things only because Jesus absorbed all the bad things from us into himself when he died on the cross. That means God can bless sinful people without compromising himself.

In other words, if Christ had not shed his blood, there could be no grace for you, me, or anybody. The Cross of Christ is the key that unlocks the door of God's grace.

Most Christians get that, at least a little bit. So they go along thinking they've got grace all figured out.

But they don't. They don't have grace figured out. They've never even graduated out of grace's preschool.

So that's what we're doing: graduating to deeper, stronger, truer levels of grace.

And you'll always be stunted in your growth till you experience...

The Security Breakthrough

Big Idea: God himself bears all the burden to keep you saved forever.

Once you're saved, you're always saved. That's the beauty of grace. For many people it's shocking to read it. It's objectionable. It leads to sin, they say.

And they would be wrong.

Peter explains that you are "kept" by the power of God forever (1 Peter 1:5). That word, *kept*, means "shielded." It means to post armed guards around someone. That's what God has done for you. God stands guard over your salvation.

Who can defeat him?

Sin can't. The devil can't. You can't. The demons can't. Your mistakes can't. Your addictions can't. Your rap sheet can't. Your in-laws can't. Your ex- can't. And God won't. Consider yourself secured forever within the invincible arms of God.

God is stuck with you forever. God is happily stuck with you.

It was grace that got you saved.

And it will be grace that keeps you saved for all the ages long.

Follow up idea: Until you feel secure in the grip of God's grace, you won't feel secure at all.

I was saved when I was a little kid. I don't remember it very well, and I don't know the date. That's okay because God remembers.

But I had a big problem. Every time I sinned, I thought I had to be saved again. I felt guilty over my sins. I always felt like I was in trouble with God, and he was going to smash me with his heavenly fly swatter.

So I did what any self-respecting, adorable, little Italian boy would do: I got saved again. And again and again and again.

Even though my Awana leaders and Sunday school teachers said my salvation was forever, I never felt secure about that.

It's another one of those cases where what I believed in my head, didn't really affect what I felt in my heart.

My psychology had not caught up with my theology, so both were shaky.

I was sure that one day, I would stand all alone before God. I would grovel and cringe and be embarrassed as he threw my sins back in my face. I thought he would broadcast all my secret guilt and shame on his massive flat screen heavenly high-def screen for all the universe to see... and then maybe, just maybe, he would roll his eyes, and let me into heaven with as much enthusiasm as a dog giving up a bone.

I did not feel secure in the grip of God's grace at all. I was sure he would let me fall.

That spiritual insecurity became emotional insecurity. I didn't feel good about myself. I always felt I had something to prove. I had to do more for Jesus. I had to work harder, and sweat sweatier to earn the approval of God. I had to live for the Kingdom or else.

That is the opposite of grace.

It is impossible to feel secure in yourself if you don't feel secure in God. That's how God made us. It's how we're wired. Until you feel secure in the grip of God's grace, you won't feel secure at all.

> So we may boldly say: "The Lord is my helper; I will not fear. What can man do to me?" (Hebrews 13:6)

You know you've made your security breakthrough when you can say "the Lord is my helper, I will not fear, what can the people around me do to me..." and when you can actually say that boldly.

The voice of legalism says, I'm stuck being God's helper. The voice of grace says, the Lord is MY helper.

The voice of legalism says, I can never be quite sure about God's love. The voice of grace says, I will not fear!

The voice of legalism says, Other people's opinion defines my life, and dominates my life, and hurts my life! People are stronger in my life than God. The voice of grace says, What can people do to me?

I want you to really notice what's going on in this verse.

The Lord is my helper... that's a theological statement. That is the posture God takes in your life.

The Lord is my helper. That is theology.

I will not fear... that is psychology.

So that we may boldly say... that is also psychology.

What can people do to me... that is also psychology.

Grace lives at the intersection where the Bible's theology meets your psychology.

You can sing Amazing Grace. You can teach grace. You can say, "I know all about grace." You can trace the river of grace back to its headwaters in the Cross of Christ. You can know the theology quite well.

But until you *feel* secure in the grip of God's grace, you're only scratching the surface. You really have some grace-growing to do. You need a thousand ready answers to a thousand lies the devil's going to hit you with against the love of God.

It's one thing to nod your head, and say, Yes, I have eternal security. Once I'm saved, I'm always saved... but then all your crazy insecurities keep running your life. What's that about?

The basic idea of this chapter is simple: ALL insecurities that dominate your life are traceable to your insecurities about God. There's a lie hidden beneath your insecurities. It says that there is something you can do or not do that will make God stop being faithful to you.

Let's consider three big insecurities that don't need to run your life for one more second. They are like blood sucking vampires... when you hold up the power of the Cross, these insecurities will turn and run away.

Insecurities

1. Abandonment

The best dog I ever owned was a black lab mutt I got from a shelter, named Jesse. Sadly, he went to doggie heaven a few years go. We were extremely attached. Wherever I was, there Jesse had to be in the midst.

My little house in Chicago was a long skinny lot, and the house was set toward the back of the lot. I had a big front lawn. There was a little fenced yard by the house.

One day, I put Jesse in the yard so I could mow the lawn. I fired up the lawn mower and got to work. I pushed the lawn mower away from the house, and away from the fenced area where Jesse was stuck. He went nuts. Whining and pawing and howling and crying, just because I was walking away from him. I'm sure Jesse was thinking, "This is just like the people who abandoned me to the shelter the first time. Here we go again."

He was really miserable.

Then I reached the end of the yard. I turned around and started mowing back toward the house. Jesse's tail wagged, and he smiled and got very happy. He must have thought, "He likes me! He really likes me!"

And then I reached the end of the grass, and turned around again to mow the next strip going the other way. What do you think Jesse did?

He started whining again. He's leaving me! Panic! Don't leave me!

And back and forth for the whole lawn.

Jesse had abandonment issues.

All I could think was... *You silly dog. I'm just making the yard nicer for you, and you're freaking out about it.*

God says, "Do not fear." He calls himself *your helper.* Helper. Let that sink in. He will not abandon you. He will not forsake you. He will not leave you. A helper doesn't abandon the person he helps.

You have a Father in heaven who never skips town, never ignores you, and never forgets your need.

He won't abandon you even if you sin.

He won't abandon you even if you fail.

He won't abandon you even if you go through tough times.

He won't abandon you even if you abandon him.

No matter what human has abandoned you, God has not abandoned you. He can't.

That's because on the day you became a Christian, God made you one with Christ. You are one with Christ, joined to him, super-glued to him forever.

Question: when will God abandon Jesus Christ?

Answer: never.

Then he will never abandon you either. For God to be unfaithful to you he'd have to be unfaithful to Christ. Can't happen.

Whatever insecurities about abandonment tear at your soul, they do not and cannot come from God.

It could have been your earthly father. It could have been your mother or your spouse or your lover. It could have been a severe loss early in your life. Sometimes people are so afraid of being abandoned, they decide to check out first—they become the "abandoner."

Let the Holy Spirit, by the Word of God, explode the lie that God will abandon you now that you belong to Christ.

The Lord is your Helper, and he will never leave you alone.

Rest secure in a love that never fails.

2. Acceptance

Will people like me? Will I fit in? Will people think I'm weird? Will I get to sit with the cool kids, or will I be voted off the island?

You can trace all your human insecurities to your insecurities about God.

Will God like you? Will God think you're weird? Will God vote you off his heavenly island?

Here's a tremendously healing promise from God:

> To the praise of the glory of His grace, by which He has made us accepted in the Beloved. (Ephesians 1:6)

You are accepted in the Beloved. Let's decode this.

The Beloved, with a capital B, is another title for Jesus Christ.

So you are accepted "in Jesus Christ."

Let's decode that some more.

"In Jesus Christ" is the Bible's way of talking about you becoming one with Christ.

So here we are cracking the code:

God accepts you because God accepts Jesus Christ, and when you were saved, you became one with him.

Listen, the cool kids at school might not like you, but God does. The other ladies might not include you in their adventures, but God includes you. God feels the same way about you that he feels about Jesus. He thinks you're awesome. He believes in you more than you believe in yourself.

Some time ago, I attended a major pastors' conference. I can be pretty confident at times. I can also be pretty insecure. I didn't know anybody at this conference, and nobody knew me. So all these guys were friends, and they were laughing, and hanging around, and having a good time.

And there I was, a floater, drifting from conversation to conversation trying to fit in. I felt like a middle school introvert getting shoved into a new school.

"Um... hi. I'm Bill. So what's your sign?"

It was painful.

All of a sudden, there was a commotion near the entrance. The main leader of this whole conference arrived. People moved his direction, and crowded around him.

I had a secret: I had been his student in seminary and he liked me. A lot. He actually asked me to date his daughter. Truth. (Note: I was single at the time.)

The speaker saw me through the crowd across the room. He yelled, "Bill!" and he ran over, gave me a bear hug, and introduced me to the guest speaker that everybody had come to hear. I shook hands with this national speaker who's been on the news and was a household name.

And then the speaker said, "Bill, I want you to sit at my table when we eat..." So he brought me over to his table, and sat me right between him, and this big time speaker.

Now, all these guys who didn't know me at all were thinking, "So that's Bill."

I sat there thinking I'm pretty cool.

I also whispered a prayer: "For the love of everything holy, please don't let me dribble food on my shirt."

The minute the Big Guy accepted me, I was in. I didn't have to be popular with everybody; just with the Big Guy.

If you are a Christian, the Biggest Guy of all has accepted you. Perfectly. Totally.

You can't ruin that.

The mean girls can't ruin that.

The bullies can't ruin that.

Your own failures can't ruin that.

Your spouse or your ex- can't ruin that.

Your sins can't ruin that.

And for the rest of eternity, when your Father in heaven thinks of you, he will smile ear to ear, and he will say, "Bill [insert your name there] you are my child, and you are precious to me."

This is the grace of God.

Be secure.

3. Appearance

Insecurity around *appearance* rises like Godzilla to devour most in our culture today.

Our kids are most vulnerable: You're ugly. Too fat. Too skinny. Too short. Too tall. Bad complexion. Bad eyes. Bad shape. You're not healthy. You don't wear makeup. You don't have a boyfriend yet. You don't have a girlfriend yet. You don't talk right. You smell funny.

You're clothes are cheap. Your shoes are so yesterday. You have a bad complexion, bad hair, bad breath, uncool voice.

Every magazine cover shows a perfect, million-dollar body that's been Photoshopped to produce a superhuman image that a mere mortal like you could never, in a million years of diet and exercise, come close to.

A little voice inside your head says, "I'm not good enough."

Boom! Another insecurity has just taken root.

What do you do with it?

You can go a couple of directions. Some people will go crazy trying to wear the costume of coolness. They'll spend money, buy the right clothes, starve themselves, and do all kinds of sad things in order to feel secure over how they look.

Other people will just give up. They'll dress to not be noticed. They'll slouch to make themselves small. They make themselves invisible because at least that way nobody can hurt them.

I get you, I understand you.

Our culture has raised appearance to a ridiculously important level, and it makes no sense at all.

Appearance doesn't heal diseases.

Appearance doesn't comfort those who hurt.

Appearance doesn't fix anybody's broken down car.

Appearance doesn't teach classrooms.

Appearance doesn't embrace hurting children.

Appearance doesn't do anything important for the welfare of humankind at all.

Because appearance is just an arrangement of the same body parts we all share.

Real beauty lies within your heart. If somebody in your life doesn't get that, they just don't belong in your inner circle.

The only reason physical beauty is such a big deal is this: *we swim in a sea of craziness.* So stupid, sick, dysfunctional people are leading our culture down a hyper-sexualized, hyper-monetized, hyper-deperson-alized path that has dehumanizing values, warped morals, and always leads to broken hearts.

Yes, do your best with what you've got. Get as clean as you can and look as nice as you can without driving yourself crazy. But never base your security on how good looking other people say you are.

That will only distract you from how beautiful God says you are.

> You shall no longer be termed Forsaken, Nor shall your land any more be termed Desolate; But you shall be called Hephzibah, and your land Beulah; For the LORD delights in you, And your land shall be married. (Isaiah 62:4)

Let's decode this, especially the Hebrew words Hephzibah and Beulah. Here's what it all means:

Just when you feel totally rejected, just when you feel totally unloved, God swoops in, and sweeps you off your feet and he says you're beautiful to him.

He calls you *Hephzibah*, which means you make God happy whenever he looks at you.

He calls you *Beulah*, which means you are beautiful to him, like a bride or groom dressed for your wedding day.

He says you are *Not Forsaken*; you are married to God. He delights in you.

How did he come to see you this way?

Christ washed you. Christ performed a spiritual makeover on you, and whatever ugliness marred your beauty has been swept away. He robed you in glorious robes of beauty. He decked you in absolute perfection.

When Christ was crucified, he absorbed whatever ugliness clung to you. He buried it forever in a sea of forgetfulness.

So now you are perfect in God's eyes.

No matter what you do or don't do or start doing or stop doing.

It's grace.

Be secure.

Your sins won't stick to you. You're tears won't make you ugly to God. The marks on your body, the weakness in your bones, the failure of your systems, the brokenness mapped in your eyes, and the sadness of your smile... none of these change the fact of your beauty in the eyes of God. His heart melts over you. He rejoices over you with "leaps of joy" (Zephaniah 3:17).

Christ holds your hand, and his radiance lights up the magnificent beauty in you that will one day make angels bow at your feet.

All your insecurities should fade into oblivion whenever you look into your Father's eyes. If you could fly to heaven and see for ten seconds the warm smile of infinite love, and tenderhearted compassion he has for you, you'd never feel insecure again.

Be secure.

You are beautiful to God.

You are accepted by God.

You will never be abandoned by him.

Eternal Security:
The Ultimate Security Breakthrough

Eternal Security is the teaching that says once you're saved, you're always saved.

Even if you sin.

Even if you invent a new sin nobody ever did before.

Even if you cross a boundary you promised you would never cross.

Grace means that the work of keeping you saved is as much God's job as the work of getting you saved. God bears that burden. Only he can.

Heaven is not a merit badge for people who behave.

Heaven is a gift for people who believe.

Eternal security. That's not just a statement of how long your salvation endures, though that's part of it. You have an eternal salvation, and for all the millions of eternal ages, you will swim in an ocean of grace that will never cease to amaze.

But it's not just how long your salvation endures.

It's also how deep your salvation goes. *Eternal...* how long your salvation endures. *Security...* how deep your salvation goes.

Right down into your psychology.

Right down into your dysfunction and fears and anxieties and insecurities.

Be secure.

The Lord is my Helper. Say it boldly. Don't whisper it. Don't say it timidly. Don't doubt it. Own it. Claim it. Stand on it.

The Lord is My helper... The Lord is my security. The Lord is my ever-present help in time of need.

This is your security breakthrough.

> So we may boldly say: "The LORD is my helper; I will not fear. What can people do to me?" (Hebrews 13:6)

Prayer

Almighty God,

You took hold of my hand the day you saved me, and you have never let me go. You will never let me go. And you can never let me go, because you promised to walk me all the way home to you.

Lord, break through my insecurities. When I worry about your love for me, hold me close. When fears of the future gather on the horizon, tower over them. When I question my salvation, assure me by your Spirit and your Word. When I feel the need to hide from you, wipe it away, and help me believe your invitation to come boldly to you.

I rest all my anxieties in you, and I claim by faith the utter, eternal, and irrevocable security in which I stand by grace alone.

Through Christ's Great Love,

Amen.

4

THE IDENTITY BREAKTHROUGH

Therefore we were buried with Him through baptism into death, that just as Christ was raised from the dead by the glory of the Father, even so we also should walk in newness of life. For if we have been united together in the likeness of His death, certainly we also shall be in the likeness of His resurrection. (Romans 6:4, 5)

Nothing is more central or basic than union and communion with Christ.... Union with Christ...in its broader aspects underlies every step of the application of redemption. Union with Christ is really the central truth of the whole doctrine of salvation not only in its application but also in its once-for-all accomplishment in the finished work of Christ. Indeed the whole process of salvation has its origin in one phase of union with Christ and salvation has in view the realization of other phases of union with Christ. -John Murray

BIG LIE #4: I MUST STAY BUSY FOR JESUS TO PROVE MYSELF TO GOD AND OTHERS.

GRACE IS THE UNDESERVED favor of God; the goodness that flows from God to us without us doing even one little thing to earn it.

Grace is almost too good to be true. But it is true, because it's in the Bible.

There's this funny reaction that people have to grace.

It's almost like a new word has been invented. It's the word, "yes-but."

"Okay, I agree with everything you're saying about grace, BUT you still have to... [fill in the blank: bear fruit, be holy, stop sinning, and on and on.]" A grace-yes-but.

Another example: "Okay, Jesus died for our sins, and he did everything to save us... yes... but... we still have to do our part."

Grace has no yes-buts.

You know you have made a grace breakthrough when you are finally able to resist the incredible urge to yes-but grace. Grace has no yes-buts, because, almost always, "yes-but" means NO.

It makes me laugh that, whenever I post something about grace on Facebook, invariably somebody's going to comment with some kind of yes-but. Count on it.

I also know, that right now, you may be thinking, "yes-but, what you're saying right now needs a yes-but." That's exactly my point. Earlier, we saw how the human heart is blind to its own resistance to grace. We don't come into grace naturally. We come kicking and screaming. Arguing and yes-butting. We need an intervention. We need some kind of shock to the system to break through the resistance.

Grace has no yes-buts.

I understand the concern: too many people call themselves Christians but don't really live the life of a Christian. So many Christians use grace to excuse their bad behavior.

It is a real problem, but *quit blaming grace.* If anything, blame the awful scourge of GDD — Grace Deficit Disorder. The thing that makes Christians behave badly isn't grace; it's a deficiency of grace.

Scandalous Grace

Grace is the most counterintuitive force in the universe. It is the heartbeat of Jesus Christ. It is the opposite of human assumptions, the antithesis of human worthiness, and the absolute rival of any religion ever devised by the fallen mind of humankind.

When Jesus taught grace, he scandalized people. He agitated the legalists. They fired back their yes-buts. When he taught grace, people got mad. He didn't water it down, didn't pollute it with works, and didn't let even one single yes-but stick.

He just let grace hang out there, naked, and scandalous. That drove religious people crazy. That's how Jesus knew he got his point across.

His disciples and apostles picked up where he left off. Paul wrote, "But by the grace of God I am what I am..." (1 Corinthians 15:10). Here was a highly educated, passionate, devoted, follower of God. A true rising star. He clawed his way to the top. An over-achiever. A workaholic. A bona-fide success story. He'd climbed to the top of his culture's ladder.

Only to discover it was leaning against the wrong wall.

So he jumped down and let Jesus carry him up the right wall. Only when Jesus deposited him at the top, could he survey the vistas of Calvary's love and the wonders of God's goodness... and then declare, "But by the grace of God I am what I am..."

What magic sauce did Paul have in his soul to make a statement like that?

When God's grace broke through it blew his mind. That grace reordered his entire sense of self. I am what I am... by the sweat of my brow? ...by the genetic hand I was dealt? ...by the luck of the stars? ...by the pestilence of my insane/criminal/dysfunctional family tree?

No.

I am what I am by the grace of God.

You don't like it? The true me? The real me? The person I am in Christ? You're not a fan?

So what!

When your identity rests on grace, nobody can define you. Nobody can defeat you or dominate you. Let's think about this Identity Breakthrough, truth by truth.

Five Truths

1. People act out of who they are.

You act out of who you are. You act out of your sense of self. Your identity. Who you believe yourself to be.

- "Keep your heart with all diligence, For out of it spring the issues of life" (Proverbs 4:23).
- "For as he thinks in his heart, so is he..." (Proverbs 23:7a).

For good or bad, your actions, behaviors, words, and instincts flow from the fountain of your identity. The "Who Am I?" question never loses its power.

God told Moses to set his people free. Moses said, "Who am I?" because he saw himself as damaged goods (Exodus 3:11).

God told Jeremiah to go speak for him as a prophet. Jeremiah said, "I can't, 'for I am a youth'" (Jeremiah 9:6).

The stuff you do isn't random. There's always logic to it. It comes from somewhere. Life projects the heart. Jesus lamented the dark side of this reality: "For out of the heart proceed evil thoughts, murders, adulteries, fornications, thefts, false witness, blasphemies" (Matthew 15:19).

People act outwardly out of who they see themselves to be inwardly.

As a pastor, I have to live in this reality. I can't just preach against people's bad behavior and expect lasting change. It won't work to only teach practical steps showing how to change stuff in your life—for example, how to heal dysfunctional finances—without first addressing a person's sick relationship with *self* that's squirting out into the outer world as fiscal insanity.

Revival will come when the people of God across the land embrace their true identity—the labels God puts on them now that they belong to Christ.

Who are you?

Don't just tell me your name, your city, your job, your resume. Who are you, in your heart of hearts? Because that core self sits behind a curtain pulling the levers on the life you ultimately create.

[For further study: see my book *Grace Rehab*, where we dig into seventeen "I Am" statements about a Christian's new identity in Christ.]

2. You've been slimed.

Let me illustrate how that works.

> *A true story:* I saw it with my own eyes, I felt it in the pit of my own stomach. I can still feel it.

The place: the crowded cafeteria in my large, urban high school. At that time, the student body hovered around five-thousand. Picture a cavernous hall. It's old. It's worn out. It's institutional gray. The sounds of hungry students echo off hard tile floors and cold Formica tables. It smells like stale food mingled with sweat.

The scene: a table full of guys was taunting a girl. She was just trying to put away her lunch tray in peace. The guys released their verbal torpedoes, while sitting at their table. Just words.

"Hey Susan, how did you get so ugly?"

"You're hideous!"

"Your mother should have drowned you when you were born!"

"Hey, Ugly!"

The taunts shot across the room and hit her like punches. The whole lunchroom paused to watch. It was horrible.

Susan's head dropped. She fought back tears. She pretended not to hear.

I knew her a little bit. She just wasn't into makeup and fashion and all that. She was very smart—an excellent student and a very nice person.

That didn't matter. Once the sadists in the cafeteria got started, nothing stopped them.

Susan ducked as a coleslaw cup whizzed by and splatted against the wall. She couldn't take any more. Her face distorted by agony, she turned to her attackers and screamed. "Shut up! Shut up! Shut up!"

It was like dripping blood into shark-infested waters, Susan's reaction sparked a feeding-frenzy. The boys called her a dog and started howling—like wolves baying at the moon.

My stomach tied in a knot that would take hours to untie. I didn't feel safe.

Susan ran from the lunchroom, refusing to give anybody the satisfaction of seeing her cry.

I left too, and went on with my classes. Just another day in the big city, public school jungle.

I felt wounded, just for witnessing it. I don't pretend to imagine the devastation that Susan felt for living it.

[Excerpted from *Grace Rehab*, used by permission.]

You've been slimed. You've probably collected your share of labels as you've gone through life. Some are overtly slapped on you: stupid, ugly, fat, worthless, and worse. Mean girls and bullies, stoned out parents and heartless teachers—like flies on road kill, they buzz around your heart's deep wounds.

Other labels aren't so overt. The disapproving glance. The relentless stream of corrections masquerading as "suggestions." A painful withholding of affection. Somehow, the message gets through that you aren't worthy, aren't capable, or simply will never measure up.

Watch an hour of television and you'll discover how ugly you are. There's just no way to measure up to the polished beauty and chiseled muscularity you see. Don't quite have a "Beachbody"? Best bag it in bulky clothes and slouch so as not to be noticed.

Slimed.

You can't avoid it. The whole world is infected. The Evil Labelmaker from hell spews toxic slime across us all. The whole world lies "under his sway" (1 John 5:19). TRANSLATION: we're all in his spit zone.

These labels sink deep inside a person. They latch onto your tender spirit. They haunt you. They define you.

And that's where your inner mess begins to trash your outer world.

3. The labels you embrace create self-fulfilling prophecies.

Joe's parents called him STUPID every time he failed. Without a breakthrough, what kind of life will he create?

Misha's peers called her a LOSER after she froze during a classroom presentation. The label stuck throughout high school. She heard it ten thousand times. Without a breakthrough, how will she rise above that label?

Sally grew up in a wealthy home as Daddy's little princess. Every day, he told her she was BETTER THAN everyone else. Without a breakthrough, how could she grow up without being hyper-competitive and fragile when she fell short of perfection?

If you embrace the label that you're ENTITLED, you're going to be a high-chair tyrant, and a professional victim.

The outside we all see is always a projection of the inside we don't see.

Whatever strength you have flows out of the inner strength in your sense of self.

Whatever dysfunction you have flows out of the dysfunction in your sense of self.

Who knows the real you?

God.

On your good days, you do too.

Other than that, the rest of us are guessing. Our guesses are based on what we see and hear. While anyone can fake it for a while, over the long haul, your lifestyle will always incarnate whatever self-identifying labels you embrace.

You just can't avoid it.

If you were one of the blessed few who grew up in a healthy home with positive parents and good-hearted friends, I'm happy for you.

And a little jealous.

For the rest of us, we have to come to grips with the fact we've been slimed with a toxin that seeps into relationships, sexuality, finances, self-esteem, and every nook and cranny of our identity.

So now what?

So now God has to bring us through an Identity Breakthrough.

That's where grace comes in.

4. Grace rehabs your identity first.

Nothing cleanses the slime of a broken identity like the flood of Calvary's love.

Jesus peeled off every nasty label and ran it through the shredder of the Cross. Then he atomized the shreds and blew them as far away from you as the east is from the west. When Christ died on the cross, he removed once for all every demeaning label ever slapped upon you by anybody, past, present, or future.

That was real, theologically.

Now, God's Spirit goes to work on you to heal your sense of self, psychologically. Grace heals the identity first. In heaven, Jesus says he will write on you a "new name" (Revelation 3:12).

So what, if the mean girls name you Ugly?

Who cares if your mother-in-law names you Incompetent?

The bullies who named you Wimp, the father who named you Nobody, the mother who named you Stupid... they have nothing to say to you. You don't need to spend one nano-second proving yourself to any of them.

Your new name has been cemented by Christ, and it is glorious.

All the rest are powdery lies, blown into hell with the devil where they belong.

You are a new person, with a new name, and a new identity linked to the identity of Jesus Christ. You have been joined to Christ. You are one with Christ. You are in permanent union with Christ. He covers you with his robe of righteousness, and clothes you in his glory. If you are saved, you are in Christ. That is the true you, the real you, the only you, forever.

Let it sink in.

Pray through it.

Claim it.

Say it out loud: "I am who God says I am, and he says I am just like Christ."

Grace rehabs your identity first.

And you've got nothing left to prove to God or anybody.

5. God rehabs your identity by joining you to Christ.

On the day you received Jesus as your Savior, God did something irreversible: he joined you to Jesus Christ. He superglued you to Christ. You became one with him. The Bible says you were married to Christ, joined to Christ, baptized by the Holy Spirit into Christ (Romans 7:4, 1 Corinthians 6:17, Romans 6:3-6).

Before meeting Jesus, I was plain, solitary Bill. Just me. Bill plus zero.

Now that I have Jesus as my Savior, I am Bill plus Christ forever. I've been fused to him, so to speak. My old identity is gone—Bill plus zero no longer exists. Only the new one remains, Bill plus Christ. As weird as it might sound, this is a very good thing.

The Bible uses the words "in Christ" or "in him" to indicate this. Here's one of many examples: "There is therefore now no condemnation to those who are in Christ Jesus..." (Romans 8:1). To be in Christ is to be totally free from condemnation, once for all.

See how that works?

Buckle your seat belt, because the implications are astounding. You are so joined to Jesus Christ that whatever God says about Jesus, he now says about you.

If God were to describe you today, what would he say? If he were to stand up in the throne room of heaven, command the silence of the worshipping angels and feasting saints, and say, "Today, I'm going to tell you all about [insert your name here,]" what would that celestial speech sound like?

If you are in Christ, he would describe you in the same terms he would use to describe Jesus.

What does God say about Jesus? Is he beautiful? Is he acceptable? Is he valuable? Is he powerful?

Then you are too.

What would God never say about Jesus? I hate you? I don't want you? You're ugly? Leave me alone? You're stupid? No, of course not, never in a million times a million millennia. It's unthinkable.

If he would never say those things about Jesus, then he would never say, or even think, those things about you. You are one with Christ.

When God joined you to Christ, he erased every demeaning label that every schoolyard bully, every mean girl, every stoned parent, and every religious hypocrite ever spray-painted across your heart. You are not ugly. You are not stupid. You are not worthless. You are not anything the world says you are.

You are who God says you are.

And he says you are in permanent union with the best person whose leather sandals ever trudged the dusty streets of planet earth.

How Do People Change?

There are two answers to that question:

The legalistic answer says that the way to make people be like Jesus is by telling them what to do or stop doing. Or by informing them *how* to do what Jesus said to do. The legalistic answer lives at the behavioral level only.

Here's an example: The Bible tells husbands to love their wives. So I'm talking to a husband, and I tell him — "Sir, be a good man and love your wife."

He says, "Sure. I'll try that. Got any pointers?"

I say, "Buy some flowers, take care of some of the chores she normally takes care of, speak with kindness, and go on a surprise date."

He says "Great!" and goes home to try it.

All my suggestions are at the behavioral level.

But here's the fatal flaw.

What if that man hates himself?

What if that man still cowers before the inner demons of a violent father, or an alcoholic mother? What if he seethes with rage and self-punishment? What if he's convinced that God is against him?

What if that man hates himself? How will he ever love his wife well?

All my practical tips only drive him deeper into despair over what a horrible person he is. So, during his big date night with his wife, he gets embarrassed by something trivial, lashes out, throws the flowers on the floor, and acts like a bigger jerk toward her than ever before.

Why?

Because people act out of who they are. And who he is, in his mind, is just a weakling wandering through a war zone who's got to prove himself through fighting.

How can he ever be like Jesus?

Here's how: *Grace rehabs the identity first.*

How do Christians become Christlike? The legalistic answer would say by giving people a list of do's and don'ts and telling them to obey.

"Just do it."

Here's the grace answer:

In the grace answer, the way to help people change is by filling their hearts with their riches and identity in Christ.

So this man, who can't be kind to his wife, needs to see himself in the mirror of Scripture. He needs to be taught:

- You label yourself, NOT WORTHY, but God labels you "qualified to be a partaker of the inheritance of the saints in light" (Colossians 1:12).
- You label yourself, SINNER; Christ shouts back SAINT.
- You label yourself, ADDICT; Christ shouts back REDEEMED.
- You label yourself, DIRTY; Christ shouts back, "Washed in the blood of the Lamb!"
- You label yourself, GUILTY; Christ shouts back FORGIVEN.
- You label yourself a fatherless child, and God labels himself Father to the fatherless and makes you his child (Psalm 68:5, John 1:12).
- You label yourself worthless, and he labels you precious (Isaiah 43:4).
- You label yourself hateful, and he labels you beloved (Ephesians 1:6).

- You label yourself stupid and incompetent, and he labels you "able to do all things" (Philippians 4:13).
- You label yourself fat, or tall, or skinny, or blemished, or ugly, or broken, and he labels you GLORIOUS (Colossians 3:4).
- You label yourself as lost and forgotten, and he says, "Can a woman forget her nursing child, neither will I forget you... behold, I have engraved you on the palms of my hands." (Isaiah 49:15,16).
- You label yourself a waste of a life, and he labels you an invincible soldier on a mission from heaven (Titus 2:3,4).

So I teach all that to that Husband. That Angry Man. That Wounded Spirit. I patiently bring grace to his soul. Over and over again.

Finally, three weeks later, for the first time in a long time, he actually says a kind word to his wife. That's because, for the first time in his life, he's starting to feel good about himself. He's finally seeing himself as God sees him.

Grace rehabs the identity first, because people act out of who they are.

And telling them how to act won't change anything for the long term without saturating their spirits with who God says they are in Christ.

This is your Identity Breakthrough.

Do you copy?

Because if who you are in Christ routinely gets swamped by who other people say you are, it means you haven't learned grace deeply enough. You have Grace Deficit Disorder, and it's going to hurt your life, your marriage, your dating, your sexuality, your children, your relationships, your finances, and your church.

The beautiful thing with God is that he makes all things new. It doesn't have to be this way. Life doesn't have to stay broken. You can lay hold of all that for which Christ laid hold of you (Philippians 3:12). You really can.

Discover who you are in Christ, and weave it into the fabric of your soul. Remember grace lives at the intersection where theology meets psychology.

Remember the logic:

People act out of who they are.

You've been slimed.

The labels you embrace create self-fulfilling prophecies.

Grace rehabs your identity first.

We're talking about an identity breakthrough. Here's the last big truth, and here's where I get you upset:

5. Please stop serving God.

All the legalists reading this just said, "I knew it! Heretic!"

Some just heard a voice inside say, "Yes-but."

Remember, you are infected with resistance to grace. It is very possible you have Christianity backwards and don't know it.

Jesus said,

> "I am the vine, you are the branches. He who abides in Me, and I in him, bears much fruit; for without Me you can do nothing." (John 15:5)

There are two sides to Christ's teaching here.

Side one, abide in Christ.

Side two, bear much fruit.

Most Christian preaching and writing commands the Church to go forth and bear fruit. We even list the fruit-making opportunities in the church bulletin. We give tips on how to craft the fruit. We flog people into producing the fruit. Then we judge them for not bearing fruit fast enough.

We make everything about you serving God, helping God, doing for God, and cooking for God, almost to the point where God is dependent on you.

But remember that little verse where God says, "I am your helper?" (Try saying that out loud while emphasizing the pronouns "I" and "your".)

When we preachers talk about fruit all the time, we're skipping something, right?

"Abide in me."

That's what we're missing. That's what the church forgets. That's what preachers stopped talking about a generation ago. That's basically what this whole book is about.

Abide in Christ.

How?

Jesus had dinner at the home of Martha and Mary. Martha worked in the kitchen. Mary hung out with Jesus. Which one was serving God?

Martha.

Which one did Jesus praise?

Mary!

You say, How's that fair?

Welcome to grace. It's backwards from what you think. Stop serving God, Martha. Get out of the kitchen and start abiding in Christ, and you will bear much fruit.

Like an iceberg, most of that fruit will be invisible till God mostly heals your broken, wounded heart. That's fruit too. That healing. That internal rewiring. That grace rehab. That's fruit too.

Abide in Christ. Rest in him. Discover him. Learn your riches and identity in him. Revel in your security. Feast at the table of grace.

Start by climbing into his lap, and letting him tell you who exactly who you really are.

Do You Know?

Do you know who you are? Do you feel your identity? Do you snap out of it when you're tired? Do you grow irritable?

- You were lost; you are now found.
- You were in darkness; you are now in the light.
- You were alienated; you are now reconciled.
- You were in your sins; you are now forgiven.
- You were without righteousness; you are now declared righteous.
- You were condemned; you are now accepted.
- You were stuck; you are now redeemed.
- You were unworthy; you are now fully qualified.
- You were a child of wrath; you are now a child of God.
- You were a sinner; you are now a saint.

But of Him you are in Christ Jesus, who became for us wisdom from God--and righteousness and sanctification and redemption—that, as it is written, "He who glories, let him glory in the LORD." (1 Corinthians 1:30, 31)

Prayer

Father,

I am who you say I am. It's hard to believe it sometimes. I've heard so many different messages through my life. I've received so many heartbreaking labels. The more stressed I feel, the harder it is to believe that what you say about me is true.

But it is true. I take you at your Word. I believe you. My truest self, the real me, has been joined to Christ. I share his name. I share his nature. I share his identity. I am not what other people say I am—I am who you say I am and will be forever.

Thank you for my union with Christ.

Help me to grow deeper and deeper into my truest nature in Christ.

Through My Savior's Name,

Amen.

5

THE REST BREAKTHROUGH

And He said, "My Presence will go with you, and I will give you rest." (Exodus 33:14)

Abide in Me says Jesus. Cling to Me. Stick fast to Me. Live the life of close and intimate communion with Me. Get nearer to Me. Roll every burden on Me. Cast your whole weight on Me. Never let go your hold on Me for a moment. Be, as it were, rooted and planted in Me. Do this and I will never fail you. I will ever abide in you. -J.C. Ryle, 1800s

BIG LIE #5: GOD MAKES ME WRESTLE MY BLESSINGS OUT OF HIM.

"WE TRIED TO GET into your church, but the ushers wouldn't let us in." Two high school girls from my youth group scolded themselves for not following my church's unwritten rules. "Some men at the door told us we couldn't wear shorts to church. We're so sorry!"

The vein in my left temple throbbed. "No way!" I said. "I'm sorry. That should have never happened to you. I'm so sorry!" Our youth group had been praying for two seventeen-year old girls who had just joined the group and had never attended church anywhere.

They came—on a hot, muggy Chicago Sunday.

Two ushers-turned-bouncers stopped them dead. "Oh no. You can't come into church looking like that."

The girls turned away. Embarrassed. Feeling guilty. They told me their story that week at youth group. They blamed themselves. They felt guilty for not measuring up to God's standards.

Score one for legalism.

* * *

Anthony snorted and laughed out loud during my sermon. Later on he pulled me aside to apologize and tell his story. He'd reacted to my mention of a chapel in Italy that contained the *Scala Sancta*.

The "Sacred Stairs" were reported to be the very steps on which Jesus climbed to stand trial before Pilate. As the story goes, St. Helen, the mother of Emperor Constantine, commanded them to be dismantled, shipped to Italy, and reassembled in Rome.

For centuries, faithful pilgrims climbed up those stone stairs on aching knees, pausing to pray on each of twenty-eight marble steps. To this day, no one may stand on the Scala Sancta. Pilgrims climb up on their knees, and exit via another stairway on their feet.

For this act of self-sacrificing pain, participants are promised a full pardon from heaven for some of the suffering their sins deserve. It's called a "plenary indulgence."

When I told that story, Anthony delivered a snort on steroids. The whole audience laughed. When he apologized, Anthony told me he'd grown up in Italy. His grandmother made him climb the *Scala Sancta* every week. She would stand by weeping, wringing knobby hands, and praying for his soul.

I admire her dedication, but can't agree with her theology. Score another one for legalism.

* * *

We are all natural born legalists. We come from a long line of legalists, all the way back to Adam and Eve who sewed fig leaves to cover their shame. Instead of approaching God as empty-handed charity-cases, legalists approach him as religious success-stories who, through their hard work and sacrifice, have earned a spiritual paycheck.

"Come on, God. Pay up."

God has a way of knocking the legalism right out of us.

Case in point, Jacob. Genesis 32 tells the strange story of his wrestling match with God. I sat once at a Bible study where our teacher explained that we have to "really want" God's blessings. Like Jacob, have to "go for them" and "seize" them from the hand of God, she said. Keep wrestling till he blesses you. Anybody who wants good stuff from God better do their spiritual push-ups because he isn't Santa, and getting stuff from him isn't easy.

People cheered.

I felt queasy. Sounds like an awfully high price for an absolutely free blessing.

What exactly are the rules of God's blessings? Are blessings—like forgiveness, heaven, and daily bread—prizes God dangles just out of reach to make us jump? Is he really all that interested in the sweaty sacrifice of his hard working children?

What is the price of God's grace?

That wily rascal, Jacob, found out the hard way.

The Setup: Judgment Day

Jacob was about to collide with the brother he cheated years earlier. He was frantic. He just knew Esau was out for blood. Jacob dreaded the well-deserved hammer of justice and scrambled for a solution.

His scramble made him look like a crazy man. As Genesis has it, he bounced between legalism and grace like an Olympic ping-pong ball.

Jacob started with grace.

> Jacob said, "O God of my father Abraham and God of my father Isaac, O LORD, who said to me, 'Return to your country and to your relatives, and I will prosper you...'" (Genesis 32:9, NAS95)

He prayed to a God who promised to "prosper" him. The Hebrew word *tob*, translated "prosper" refers to God's settled disposition to do good to his people. It's a very gracious way to start a prayer.

But it gets even better.

> "I am unworthy of all the lovingkindness [*hesed*] and of all the faithfulness which You have shown to Your servant; for with my staff only I crossed this Jordan, and now I have become two companies." (Genesis 32:10, NAS95)

Hesed, beautifully translated by the word *lovingkindness,* means grace. It refers to God's policy of bestowing benefits on those who don't deserve them and haven't earned them. *Hesed* is a shining star in the Hebrew vocabulary of grace.

Jacob prayed a grace-based prayer.

Good start.

Too bad he didn't stay here.

When you're at the end of your rope, and approach God with a humble, needy heart, you're in a good place. It's called "faith." Staying there—in faith, in waiting, in trusting, in resting—is the hard part.

A little voice whispered inside Jacob's head telling him faith wasn't enough. Better pay a price.

So he slammed his heart into legalism mode and, by his actions, undercut everything he just prayed.

The Human Solution: Paying the Price Ourselves

Jacob now resorted to blatant bribery. He sent ahead treasure-laden caravans to buy his brother's forgiveness. He offered goats, camels, rams, bulls, and donkeys.

You might laugh now, but how many times have you done the same thing? How many times have you sought divine deliverance through caravans of offerings, rituals, good behaviors, self-sacrifice, and religiosity? How many times have you expected God to answer your prayers on account of a week's good behavior?

Every time we try to pay our way out of judgment or into a blessing, haven't we stepped into Jacob's dusty sandals?

Legalism thrives in the dank atmosphere of self-atonement. We may not climb up stairs on our knees, and we may not believe in religious penance, but

grades our Christian walk into a moment-by-
nance. We so easily take onto our shoulders
burden of paying for guilt—a burden that
rist can and did bear on Calvary's cross.

I've been a Christian for decades, yet still I catch myself undercutting the all-sufficiency of Christ's atoning work. I know it's stupid, but I have a mental closet crammed with fig-leaf garments I've sewn together to cover my guilt and shame. The essence of legalism is humans by human effort seeking to merit the blessing of God.

It's time for God's loving whack upside Jacob's legalistic head.

The Encounter:
Wrestling with God

Jacob prepared for dawn's showdown with his brother and his brother's militia—the fraternal Grim Reaper. He split his family into two caravans, hoping at least one would survive. He sent forth his bribe. He waited in solitude by a brook.

Enter an Unnamed Somebody who picks a fight with dispirited Jacob. Later, he will worship that Somebody, identifying him as God (v. 28).

Yes, God comes down to wrestle Jacob.

Why would God kick a guy when he's down? Isn't he supposed to be loving and kind? Why would he pick on Jacob at the lowest point in his life? Is he that uncaring?

Or could it be that he's lovingly trying to condense a lifetime of legalism into a single encounter that he might uproot it once for all?

Scripture makes the stupefying claim that puny, frightened Jacob prevailed against infinite, Almighty God (v. 25). What's going on? These Scriptures present an acted parable—depicting how legalism stretches its tentacles into every area of life with God.

First tentacle: the idea that we are on equal footing with God. Legalism, by nature, demotes God to our own mercenary level and imagines we can go nose-to-nose with him. Was Jacob actually, truly, really on equal footing with God? Not even close. God wrestled him the way a linebacker-father wrestles his five-year old kid. And, like the five-year old, legalists don't get it. Like Jacob, they imagine themselves "winners" in the eyes of God; they believe they can, by strong enough effort, squeeze a blessing out of him.

Second tentacle: the idea that we must strain ourselves to gain anything from God. Under grace, God himself bears all the burden for our blessing. Under legalism, we bear that burden. We break the sweat, pay the price, put forth the effort, and rise to an imagined level of worthiness before infinite Majesty. It's the polar opposite of the *rest* Jesus promised. Jacob expended every effort to win the wrestling match and, thus, deserve the blessing of God.

Like the girls who worried they had offended God by wearing shorts to church, our Inner Legalist frets over every sin and imperfection, worrying that God has turned against us. Instead of a grace-oriented friendship, legalism transmogrifies Christianity into a score-keeping fight with a perpetually peeved Heavenly Step-Father.

Third tentacle: the idea that if we become moral "winners" God will owe us. Legalists delude themselves into thinking that if they can only wrestle down enough temptations, and take the moral high-ground, God will suddenly become their debtor. He will owe us answered prayers, healed diseases, happy emotions, and fat wallets. Legalists conjure up their own moral "winning-ness" and morph God into a Reluctant Stepfather who only gives us what we earn.

Jacob fought to earn God's blessing.

God had to knock the legalism right out of him.

The Knockout: Human Inability and the End of Our Resources

After hours of wrestling, the Unnamed Grappler dislocated Jacob's thigh just by touching it—proof that all Jacob's winning-ness was a figment of his self-promoting imagination. No muscle-power needed at all. Just a touch, and POP! goes the socket.

It was at this point that Jacob finally flipped a spiritual switch—the same switch that God has been wrestling us all our days to flip.

He switched from *wrestling* to *clinging*.

He stopped fighting for his blessing and just held on.

Pause and let that sink in.

He stopped demanding, stopped trying to earn, win, deserve, merit, strive, or count himself worthy. Only a fool would wrestle God, and only a bigger fool would think he could win.

The moral of this story is not the victory of wrestling; it is the *victory* of *clinging*.

The victory of clinging, of giving up the fight to make yourself worthy before God.

It's the victory of trusting.

Of resting.

Of believing.

How many Christians have been confused by preachers who make a virtue out of Jacob's [delusional] wrestling!

Quit wrestling and start clinging.

Jacob switched from earning a paycheck to asking a blessing.

He switched from working to resting. From legalism to grace.

What made the difference? God dislocated his thigh. His permanent outer limp became a perpetual reminder of the very real inner limp he'd been denying all his life. He wasn't a moral winner. He wasn't a religious champion. He was a spiritual wreck who needed grace, and suddenly he understood.

The lights came on.

He clamped a death grip on God and said, "I will not let you go unless you bless me" (Genesis 32:26). That's not a claim of victory; it's an admission of defeat. It's a tapout with a plea for mercy.

To bless means to grant a favor to someone who doesn't deserve it and hasn't earned it. Blessing is the opposite of a paycheck; it is grace in action.

In that moment, Jacob died to his self-deserving ways. He died to his self-reliance. He died to "getting what I deserve" and became alive to "getting what I don't deserve." At that moment, Jacob entered the Bible's Hall of Faith.

Far from suggesting that we should somehow wrestle with God in prayer until he relents and blesses us, Jacob's life teaches the opposite. God is showing us that we've been crippled all along, and that apart from his amazing grace, we'd deserve nothing but divine retribution. Even so, his heart has been inclined to bless us all along, but our stupid claims keep getting in the way.

If you've swallowed even one bite of the devil's lie that that you have to wrestle your blessings from God, spit it out.

Flip the switch from legalism to grace. That's the real victory.

God had to dislocate his hip to make Jacob realize it.

The Rebirth: Better than You Ever Imagined

Finally, Jacob faced his day of reckoning. It was time to meet his offended brother face to face. Jacob seemed to revert to his old conniving ways when lined up the women and children in front of him, but at the last second, he "passed on ahead of them" and met Esau first. It's a radical change of plan. A radical change of approach.

No longer timid, he approaches his "judge and jury" boldly and face to face.

Grace wins.

Whew!

How did militaristic, offended brother respond? He did exactly the opposite of what Jacob expected, just as God so often does the opposite of what your low thoughts of him expect.

Grace is always counterintuitive.

In words that presage the Prodigal Son, "Esau ran to meet him and embraced him, and fell on his neck and kissed him, and they wept" (Genesis 32:4).

Jacob's bribe was irrelevant.

Jacob's wrestling was irrelevant.

Only God's gracious heart mattered.

The God we worship—the God of the Bible—runs to those who are least deserving. He is better than you think.

God's love is not for sale. God's love is not a prize given to moral winners. It is not a reward for great spiritual performances. God's love flows eternally from his heart. You don't have to wrestle it out of him. You don't need to be a moral winner. So climb down those Sacred Stairs. End your self-inflicted guilt trip. Turn away from your needless penance. Wear your shorts to church. Shed your legalistic tendencies. Walk up the sacred stairs. Heck, skip and dance up those stairs!

Call the lie a lie. No, you don't need to wrestle your blessings out of God.

Cling to Christ, through faith, boldly asking God for the blessing you need. Flip that switch from legalism to grace. And thank God that he only blesses you because of who and what he is, never because of who and what you are.

Prayer

God,

I'm tired. I'm tired of working. Tired of striving. Tired of trying to prove myself to you. I'm tired of the religious treadmill. Tired of caring what other people think.

Jesus, you said your burden was easy and your yoke was light, but I've turned my relationship with you into a miserable chore.

I'm done with that.

Today, I rest my weary soul in you. Today, I cast the burden of labor onto you and you alone. My job is faith; your job is everything else.

I rest in your character. I rest in your promises. I rest in your provision. I rest in your grace.

I rest in you.

Gratefully, in Christ,

Amen.

6

THE FREEDOM BREAKTHROUGH

Delight yourself also in the LORD, And He shall give you the desires of your heart. Commit your way to the LORD, Trust also in Him, And He shall bring it to pass. (Psalm 37:4, 5)

Christ frequently gives us the desires of our heart, though not at the particular time we desired, but a better time. –Robert Murray M'Cheyne, 1800s

Real prayer is communion with God, so that there will be common thoughts between His mind and ours. What is needed is for Him to fill our hearts with His thoughts, and then His desires will become our desires flowing back to Him. –A.W. Pink, 1900s

BIG LIE #6: GOD DOESN'T CARE ABOUT WHAT I WANT—WHAT HE WANTS IS ALL THAT MATTERS.

I AM HAUNTED BY THE TEARS of a missionary who couldn't say what he wanted. This young man had served God for eight years as a missionary in South America. He was frustrated and felt God might be leading him to another place to serve him. He didn't know what to do. He asked me for advice.

I asked him, "Well, what do *you* want?"

"Oh, I just want to do what God wants me to do... and it's so hard to figure out God's will."

"But what do *you* want to do?" I asked again.

"Well, wherever God wants me to..."

This time I interrupted him. He needed a shock. "Forget about what God wants you to do. What do *you* want? What does *your heart* want?"

He looked at me like I was an alien from Jupiter's moons. Then he burst into tears. He covered his face with his hands, and couldn't speak.

I put my arm around him. I understood him. Like him, I'd been reared with a weirdly Christianized message of "ego annihilation." What I wanted just had to be wrong; only what God wanted was right. There was a radical disconnect between the two. The fact that I wanted something made it bad.

And so another life has been sent down a miserable path of needless self-denial by the devil's torture device called legalism.

Before you start throwing rotten tomatoes, remember I am a pastor, a husband, and a father. I understand the necessity of proper self-denial. I live it every day. However, self-denial in and of itself is not a virtue: finding and living truth is. If following God's truth somewhere yields self-denial, so be it. It's the by-product, not the point, of following God's ways.

It's okay to know what you want. It's okay to give voice to that which will make you happy. Speak truth to yourself. That doesn't mean you need to pursue those things at this moment, so your beach house in Hawaii might have to wait. But at least be in touch with your wants.

Give them voice.

Know them.

If you're going to deny your wants, at least be in touch with what you're denying.

I hereby give you freedom to know what you want and to want what you want. It's okay to be free.

Freedom!

The essence of freedom is "wanting your wants." Like a sovereign king or queen, you're not afraid to say what you want. That doesn't mean you'll always get it, or even pursue it. But at least you know. You're in touch with your heart's desires.

Christ has made you free (John 8:36). Call it volition. Call it free will. God wired you this way. He made you the captain of your ship and promised to be with you wherever you might sail. Your heart's deepest desires, when you are tight with God, become a reliable guide to his will for your life.

Yes they do.

God made you free. Like a dad watching his kid ride a bike for the first time, he celebrates every hesitant movement in any direction. Love God and do what you really, deeply, passionately want, as much as that choice, a) obeys the Bible, b) keeps your word, c) honors your spouse/family (if any), and d) keeps you paying your bills.

Last year, Margi and I met with a pastor friend. He was struggling in his current position. He wondered what was next. Margi asked, "What would make *you* happy?"

He reacted viscerally. "That's not the right question. That's absolutely not the right question." He shook his head and looked into the distance. He couldn't even entertain the thought that his happiness might help him discern God's will.

Our hearts ached for him and his young family. Another victim of legalism.

Hasn't God given you dominion (Genesis 1:26, 28)? Hasn't he promised the desires of your heart (Psalm 37:4)? If you are a person of truth who loves his Word, hasn't he promised that "whatever you do will prosper" (Psalm 1:3)?

Salvation was your personal Independence Day.

Let the fireworks commence.

Legalism Kills Free Will

Legalism kills free will, or at least makes you feel guilty for using it. Here are some ways this legalism has been taught:

- Self-denial (legalistic or dysfunctional versions).
- Dying to self.
- Ego annihilation.
- Crucifying myself.
- Mortification of self (or the flesh).
- Brokenness.

These are terms I heard as part of my Christian upbringing. They made a virtue out of misery. The only time I felt good about my Christianity was when I felt unhappy. If I felt happy for too long, I was doing something wrong.

Weird, I know.

Sad, too.

The idea was that there was a radical split between what I wanted and what God wanted for me. If I wanted it, desired it, or found pleasure in it, watch out! Because "the devil always offers his second best before God offers his best."

Can you see how that would give a sincere young Christian the jitters? *Hmm... is this from the devil or from God?*

I also heard this one a lot: "Our wills must be broken to his will."

And this one too: "A snake hisses and strikes back, but a worm lets you do whatever you want."

So be a worm, because God likes you best that way.

I'm not making this up. It's a version of Christianity I was taught while growing up and it messed with my mind. It's still alive in pockets across the land.

It produces pastors, missionaries, and everyday followers of God who simply cannot voice their deepest desires without feeling guilty. They are so far out of touch with the desires of their own hearts, it feels dangerous to even name them out loud.

All of which makes the devil very happy, because it slanders the character of God.

> These things indeed have an appearance of wisdom in self-imposed religion, false humility, and neglect of the body, but are of no value against the indulgence of the flesh. (Colossians 2:23)

False Assumptions

There are several fatally false assumptions behind this teaching.

The first is that *my will and God's will never intersect.* It was just assumed that what I wanted and what God wanted were poles apart, so if I wanted to be a good Christian, I had to lay my desires on the altar of God and sacrifice them.

But what if God has a way of aligning my will with his? What if—by Christ in me, the Spirit in me, and the Word of God in me—what if God were able to transform my desires to mesh with his perfect will? Wouldn't that make following those desires a form of obedience to him (see Romans 12:1,2)?

The second fatal assumption was that *the Christian's will must be "broken,"* much as a trainer would break a horse. But what if God wanted us to be *yielded* rather than *broken*?

God, the Heart Whisperer.

I'm a father. I can't imagine "breaking" my children's wills. I want strong-willed children. I want to see resolve, firmness of intent, and true grit in them. God wants to see that in us, too. God is not interested in producing a dispirited gaggle of weak-willed wimps.

Yielded, not broken.

He wants strong-willed, feisty, big-hearted sovereigns who know what they want, want what they want, and aren't afraid to say so. Ask Moses. Ask Ruth. Ask Peter, James, and Paul. Ask Rahab. Ask Jesus.

One more fatal assumption behind the worm theology I had to shed is that *Christian freedom is just an illusion.*

If that's the case, Christ died in vain.

> Stand fast therefore in the liberty by which Christ has made us free, and do not be entangled again with a yoke of bondage. (Galatians 5:1)

What liberty? Christ as given you the freedom of an unencumbered will. It is freedom to pilot the ship of your life, and to choose your course in life within the parameters of God's Word. It is deliverance from law, from performance, from obligation, and from religion.

Liberty is knowing what you want.

It is wanting what you want.

It is saying what you want.

Even if you don't get what you want. Even if you choose to sacrifice your wants for a greater good.

It is a lie to think that what you want really doesn't matter. That is one of the devil's most noble-sounding fictions.

Dream great dreams. Pray great prayers. And pursue your dreams by the power of God's grace. Your dreams matter to God. Where do you think they came from? Don't be intimidated out of dreaming, reaching, believing.

Follow Your Heart

What is the will of God for you?

> Delight yourself also in the LORD, And He shall give you the desires of your heart. (Psalm 37:4)

Under the influence of Christ, and with a view to his glory, *do what you want.* Follow your deepest heart. God will go with you. He won't abandon you. He will bless the work of your hands. Paul said that those who have Christ "reign in life" (Romans 5:17). He put a crown on your head. You are royalty. Believe it.

Christianity is not swapping slavery to sin for slavery to God. Yes, you are God's *servant*, but only in a way that is voluntary, joyful, and unshackled. Your Master has declared you a free-born child of God. Take the helm, chart a course, and go!

Never expect under-performance from God. Dream big. Pray big. Want big. Trust a big God for mighty answers to prayer.

The day you met Jesus, the only thing you lost was the bad stuff, and the only thing you gained was the good stuff.

With pure hearts and sincere devotion to Christ, let us be free.

Prayer

Dear Lord,

I take back the scepter of my heart. I reclaim my life's throne. You gave me dominion, the devil took it away, and by faith I take it back.

Deliver me from the legalism that says my wants are irrelevant. Forgive me for making you so picky and demanding that I'm afraid to make a choice.

Lord, renew my heart, my mind, and my will. Cause me to want what you want. To desire what you desire. Align my will with yours. Revise the desires of my heart so they perfectly mesh with the desires of your heart for me.

Then open doors that lead me to fulfill those desires. Grant that I would dream your dreams for my life, and have the courage to pursue them. Do all of this by your grace, and through Christ who lives in me.

In His Name,

Amen.

THE MATURITY BREAKTHROUGH

And do not be conformed to this world, but be transformed by the renewing of your mind, that you may prove what is that good and acceptable and perfect will of God. (Romans 12:2)

Therefore, since a promise remains of entering His rest, let us fear lest any of you seem to have come short of it. (Hebrews 4:1)

Gradual growth in grace, growth in knowledge, growth in faith, growth in love, growth in holiness, growth in humility, growth in spiritual-mindedness—all this I see clearly taught and urged in Scripture, and clearly exemplified in the lives of many of God's saints. But sudden, instantaneous leaps from conversion to consecration I fail to see in the Bible. -J.C. Ryle, 1800s

BIG LIE #7: I'M SAVED, SO I'VE ARRIVED.

THERE ARE THIRTY TEAMS in Major League Baseball, fifteen in the National League, and fifteen in the American League. The National League dates back to 1876. The American League started in 1901. The two are joined together now, as Major League Baseball.

The champion is crowned by the World Series. This playoff dates back to 1901.

Moses

Rewind back in time about 3,500 years. God's people have forgotten God. The Jews are living hard lives as slaves in Egypt. God sends a deliverer named Moses. Moses reminds the people of an ancient promise from God: "you will dwell in a land flowing with milk and honey" — a prosperous land. A fertile land.

Moses reminds the Jews, "You will dwell in the Promised Land."

Let's decode "the Promised Land" into this: *a place in life where you experience maximum grace from God, and God receives maximum glory from you.*

That's what God has set before us. When you are saved, you end one journey and begin another. The one you end is the quest for forgiveness of sins and adoption into God's family. The one you begin is the quest for a maximum experience of the grace God gave you the day he saved you.

> Not that I have already attained, or am already perfected; but I press on, that I may lay hold of that for which Christ Jesus has also laid hold of me. (Philippians 3:12)

God has set before you your own Promised Land. It's what he set before the ancient Jews too.

Through Moses, God set his people free. It was a great deliverance. And off they went to the Promised Land.

It took them one year to get there.

No, not forty.

Just one, at least on their first try.

When they arrived, God said, "Way to go! You made it! Here is your Promised Land. I have given this all to you. It's an awesome place of blessing, and peace, and security, and wholeness and joy. Here is your Promised Land. Go up and possess it."

But the people whined.

They said, "But it looks so *hard*. And there are very big, scary people in the land. They look like giants. And we look like little grasshoppers. And you are so mean to us. And you're trying to kill us. And I want my Mommy."

God said, "Do not be afraid. I have given you this land. It's already yours. Go up and take it. Your victory is assured."

The people said, "It's too scary. We won't go."

"You can do it!"

"No we can't!" Sob. Sniffle. Snot bubbles.

"Yes!"

"No way, no how, too hard and scary."

God said, "What do you want to do?"

They said, "We want to go back that way."

So they wandered in the wilderness for forty years.

The World Series

Anybody who knows anything about baseball knows which team has the longest drought of winning the World Series: my beloved Chicago Cubs.

The Cubs have not won the World Series since 1908. Orville and Wilbur Wright were still flying airplanes the last time the Cubs won the World Series. There were 46 states in the USA the last time the Cubs won the World Series.

The Cubs haven't even played in the World Series since 1945, that's another record. Harry Truman was president.

It makes you wonder why a team can be so mediocre for so long.

I should say that I am a longsuffering Cubs fan, as was my father before me.

You

> So we see that they could not enter in because of unbelief. Therefore, since a promise remains of entering His rest, let us fear lest any of you seem to have come short of it. (Hebrews 3:19-4:1)

If you have received Jesus, you have crossed the ultimate threshold into the grace of God. You have moved out of slavery. Out of bondage. Out of Egypt.

One of the ways the Bible illustrates your salvation is through the Exodus. God parted the sea. The Jews were slaves to Pharaoh; you and I were slaves to sin. Through Christ, we've been set free. You've crossed the Red Sea to freedom.

But crossing the sea was not the end of the journey. Yes, it ended the journey of slavery. But now there's a new journey—one of freedom and life and joy. Now, God promises a life to you. A spiritual and emotional place to you. There's a Promised Land for you. The land is yours. Go up and take it. Possess your possessions. Take hold of your riches, and live them day by day.

We've been discovering that the teachings of grace go against nature. They are counterintuitive. You need some kind of breakthrough event to really live in the realm of grace.

One of them is a breakthrough out of a bland, vanilla, mediocre, grace-starved life of spiritual immaturity into the sunny highlands of God's grace.

The Cubs

Many of us from Chicago harbor a suspicion that explains why the team has been so mediocre for so long [until the 2016-2017 season, when they won it all—this is my hopeful prediction/prayer while writing this project].

Our suspicion is this: the Cubs don't *have* to win.

People pay good money and go to Cubs games just because it's Wrigley Field. Ivy covered walls. Nothing beats a day at the old ballpark. Great neighborhood, and a lot of awesome restaurants and nightlife.

Cubs games pretty much sell out. I'm not saying the players are bad or they don't want to win.

The ownership just knows they don't have to win.

They can coast. They can coast for a long time. They've been coasting for a very long time.

Just like some Christians we might know.

Let Us Have Grace

In the very first moment you are saved, God brings you into the realm of grace.

And now, this is what he invites you to do:

Therefore, since we are receiving a kingdom which cannot be shaken, let us have grace, by which we may serve God acceptably with reverence and godly fear. (Hebrews 12:28)

Let's take it apart.

Since we are receiving a kingdom that cannot be shaken... Since you have been brought into this grace in which you stand. Since once you're saved, you're always saved. Since you have eternal security—unshakeable security. Since you have such a rich and free and true and great and strong salvation... since everything Jesus Christ made possible through his unparalleled sacrifice on Calvary's Cross... since all his great riches have become yours, and nothing can shake you from his kingdom now or forever...

Let us have grace... Let us have and hold it. Let us cling to grace, or, more accurately, let grace cling to you. Hold to grace. Embrace this grace. Dig deeply into the wells of grace. Learn of grace. Let us grow in grace.

The writers of Scripture love to beat the drum of "possessing our possessions," of laying hold of all that is ours in Christ.

Peter said, "Grow in grace" (2 Peter 3:13).

Hebrews says, "It is good that the heart be established [made stable] by grace" (Hebrews 13:9).

God says, "looking carefully lest anyone fall short of the grace of God" (Hebrews 12:15).

When you first step into grace, you do so as a baby. You are born again as a spiritual child. God means for you to grow up. Grow mature. Grow strong. Grow stable. Grow healthy. Grow wholesome. Grow free. Grow brave.

God desires to see you become your true self—the deepest YOU with all the color added—without other people pressuring you or telling you who you are supposed to be.

He wants to unleash the Real You on a world that is starving for grace.

Why Grow?

Why grow? Why not just coast? Why not stay in spiritual kindergarten all your life?

Because God has a promised land for you. "Since a promise remains of entering His rest, let us fear lest any of you seem to have come short of it."

God has a place of rest for you to enter. What is that place? It is spiritual maturity. It is the high ground. It is the place where you experience maximum grace from God, and God receives maximum glory from you.

Spiritual maturity is that glorious place where...

You have grown past your insecurities.

You have grown past your legalism.

You have grown past your bitterness.

You have grown past your addictions and self-righteousness.

You have grown past your need to correct others and your need to get revenge.

You have grown past your temper tantrums, your violence, your deception, your unholiness, your pity parties, your professional victimhood, your immorality, your bullying, and your narcissism.

You have grown into a life of love.

And your relationships prove it.

Your heart has been established by grace. Established means stabilized. Wouldn't it be nice if you were stable? (I think your mom just shouted Hallelujah!)

I'm not saying you've mastered all these things, or that you never slip up. But the basic mode of the mature life in Christ is strong, self-assured, loving, and at peace.

It is Christ being formed in you (Galatians 4:19).

Wouldn't it be nice if people viewed you as strong and normal? You wouldn't get knocked off your feet so easily. You'd be like a tennis player, using the devil's own velocity to smash his lies back at him.

How?

"By grace" (Hebrews 13:9). By growing in grace. Learning grace. Resting in grace. And supremely by learning and thinking deeply on the cross of Jesus Christ and the grace he procured for you there.

Now that you are saved, in one sense, yes, you have arrived. But in a greater sense, your journey has just begun. There is a beautiful Promised Land waiting for you. You haven't fully arrived yet. You haven't fully experienced yet all the grace God has lavished upon you.

The devil's Plan A for your life would be that you never get saved at all. But if that fails, he switches to Plan B. Under Plan B, the devil's goal is to drag you down so that you limp beneath your true dignity, and ultimately fall short of the maximum experience of the grace of God.

Plan B infects you with the lie that once you're saved, you've arrived. Take the antidote: grow in grace.

The Wilderness

The great tragedy of the Christian church today is that so many are coasting. Wandering in the wilderness. Spiritually immature and unstable.

Forty years for the Jews back then.

A lifetime for so many today.

Some delude themselves: "I know I win in the end. I know I go to heaven. That's all I need."

Like the Cubs of years gone by, allegedly, there's no reason to put your best team on the field.

So instead of a life that feels filled with grace, you have a life that feels filled with the rough sand of the wilderness.

It's just an okay life, with an okay experience of grace, and okay godliness, and okay energy, and okay worship, and okay joy. Blandly good enough.

Coasting.

No doubt, God's grace is there even for those who coast. Even if you never grow one little bit, God's grace will never let you down. God loves babies who stay babies.

Sometimes, when we have guests over for dinner, and we can't all fit around one table, we set up an extra table for the kids. The Kiddie Table.

I remember being a kid sitting at the Kiddie Table. Good times.

But that's not what you were made for. You were made to be an ever-increasing vessel for the ever-increasing experience of God's grace.

I want this chapter to both motivate you to grow and guide you on how to do it. Here are four areas of growth for you. If you engage these four areas of growth, you'll experience a true breakthrough.

Four Growth Breakthroughs

1. Grow in Grace-promises (2 Peter 1:4).

> ...by which have been given to us exceedingly great and precious promises, that through these you may be partakers of the divine nature, having escaped the corruption that is in the world through lust. (2 Peter 1:4)

God crammed thousands of promises into the Bible for you. There's one for every circumstance of life you can imagine. Here's a small sampling. You'll find a bigger listing at the end of this book. Think of it as a spice drawer to whip up faith in different kinds of trials. Or as an ammo box to fire faith at the troubles Satan throws your way.

> *When you are afraid:* "The LORD is my light and my salvation; Whom shall I fear? The LORD is the strength of my life; Of whom shall I be afraid?" (Psalm 27:1)

> *When you are sad:* "For His anger is but for a moment, His favor is for life; Weeping may endure for a night, But joy comes in the morning." (Psalm 30:5)

> *When you have a gigantic task facing you:* "Have I not commanded you? Be strong and of good courage; do not be afraid, nor be dismayed, for the LORD your God is with you wherever you go." (Joshua 1:9)

When you feel the weight of your sins: "For as the heavens are high above the earth, So great is His mercy toward those who fear Him; As far as the east is from the west, So far has He removed our transgressions from us." (Psalm 103:11, 12)

When you feel tested/tempted: "No temptation has overtaken you except such as is common to man; but God is faithful, who will not allow you to be tempted beyond what you are able, but with the temptation will also make the way of escape, that you may be able to bear it." (1 Corinthians 10:13)

Can you see how thinking through these Scriptures can bring comfort and strength in difficult times? No matter what you're going through, there's a promise in the Bible that applies to you.

But here's a flash: you can't rely on a promise from God that you don't know.

Acres of Diamonds

There's a legendary speaker named Russell Conwell who delivered the same speech 6,152 times. He traveled around the country by horseback, and made a fortune giving his speech. He brought in millions of dollars, much of which he used to build Philadelphia's Temple University, a school still going strong over 125 years later.

What was the speech?

It was about a farmer who lived in Africa. He got tired of growing turnips, and he heard about all the diamonds people were finding in Africa. So he sold his turnip farm and went in search of diamonds. Years later, still no diamonds. He died penniless and alone.

The new farmer who bought his turnip ranch, however, was doing fine just selling turnips. One day, he picked up an interesting rock and put it on his mantel.

Some time later, a guest noticed the rock. He picked it up, and couldn't hide his astonishment. He turned to the new owner of the turnip farm, and said, "Do you know what this is?"

The farmer said, "No, I don't know what it is. But those rocks are everywhere, all over this farm. I have to keep clearing them off my fields. I have acres and acres of those rocks."

His guest nearly fainted. "These rocks, my good sir, are diamonds!"

The one sitting on the mantel turned out to be the largest diamond ever discovered to that day.

Russell Conwell's talk was called *Acres of Diamonds.*

That farmer was richer than he knew.

And you are too, assuming you know Jesus as your Savior. You hold title to Scripture's "exceedingly great and precious promises." But you can't utilize promises you don't know you have.

So what should you do?

If you want to kick your growth-in-grace breakthrough into high gear, spend some time meditating on the promises of God (listed in the back of this book). If you find one that brings comfort or joy, memorize it.

Learn it by heart, and learn its Bible address too. You're sitting on acres of diamonds and you might not even realize it. Your ignorance makes Satan rub his leathery hands together in diabolical glee.

Why not deliver a shock to his system by laying hold of the promises of God.

2. Grow in Grace-powers (Ephesians 6:10).

> Finally, my brethren, be strong in the Lord and in the power of His might. (Ephesians 6:10)

Be strong *in the Lord.* The power to be a Christian does not come from you. It can't. It has to be the power of God. Christ in you (Colossians 1:27). The Holy Spirit in you (1 Corinthians 6:19). The Word of God in you (Hebrews 4:12).

You have the power of prayer.

You have the power of the Spirit.

You have the power of your spiritual gift.

You have the power of the name of Jesus.

You have the power of the armor of God.

You have the power of peace in the midst of storms.

You have the power of whatever Scriptures you have integrated into your soul through reading, learning, listening, meditating, and memorizing.

Faith is the switch that turns on the power.

Mature faith. Weak faith. Wimpy faith, even. Any kind of faith. Scripture-built faith.

You have been so abundantly supplied with Grace-powers, that there will never be a call of God on your life to which you need to say, "I can't." The mature child of God shouts to every enemy, every adversity, and every perplexity, "I can do all things through Christ who gives me strength" (Philippians 4:13).

You may feel tired, sad, scared, broke, and weak. It doesn't matter. There is no official feeling of the power of God. Grace goes with you no matter how you feel. You can always say, "When I am weak, then I am strong" (2 Corinthians 12:10).

When ancient Israel's spiritual losers (beloved losers) came to the Promised Land the first time, and saw the giants in the way, "their hearts melted." Nothing would persuade them to take God at his word. So they wandered. They coasted. They wasted a lifetime. God still loved them. Still blessed them. Still took care of them.

But what a waste!

When they came back the second time, forty years later, an old man named Caleb stood in the war-tent with General Joshua. Caleb was 85 years old. He reached out a rough hand, put a gnarly old finger on the war-map—right on the most heavily guarded mountain, with the biggest giants, and the most heavily fortified cities. Caleb said, *"Give me that mountain!"*

It's inspiring. Read it for yourself:

> "As yet I am as strong this day as on the day that Moses sent me [to spy out the land, 40 years ago]; just as my strength was then, so now is my strength for war, both for going out and for coming in. Now therefore, give me this mountain of which the Lord spoke in that day; for you heard in that day how the Anakim [giants] were there, and that the cities were great and fortified. It may be that the Lord will be with me, and I shall be able to drive them out as the Lord said." (Joshua 14:11, 12)

That is the heart of a mature believer. No coasting. No whining. No immaturity. Just a magnificent heart stabilized by grace.

I guess we know who wasn't stuck at the Kiddie Table.

This wasn't the first time we saw Caleb in this light. Forty years earlier he was one of two of Israel's leaders who voted to go fight the giants right then and there. The other was Joshua.

This man Caleb had something big in his heart. Something invincible.

Caleb tapped into the omnipotent power of God. He knew the secret. He cracked the code. Grace wasn't just an idea, a thin layer of frosting on the surface of salvation's cake. It was the main ingredient of the whole thing. Grace gave structure to his thinking, believing, feeling, and instincts. It went bone deep. And it made him a man who rose head and shoulders above his peers.

He spit out the lie that the Exodus was all God had for him. He wanted his Promised Land. Growth in grace did that for him.

Growth in grace will do the same for you.

How do you grow in grace? Dig into the Bible. Learn the deep things of God—theology, doctrine, the whole counsel of God. Spend time in prayer. Be real. Authentic. Compassionate. Repeat. It's not rocket science.

I can't leave Caleb's story without pointing out his unfortunate name.

In the language of his day, Caleb means *dog*.

In the culture of his day, dogs were not valued. They were undomesticated scavengers. Think *rats*.

His parents named him Dog.

But Caleb possessed the heart of a world-class champion.

I guess he successfully made his identity breakthrough. And now, he's made his growth breakthrough too.

3. Grow in Grace-living (Titus 2:11-13).

> For the grace of God that brings salvation has appeared to all men, teaching us that, denying ungodliness and worldly lusts, we should live soberly, righteously, and godly in the present age, looking for the blessed hope and glorious appearing of our great God and Savior Jesus Christ." (Titus 2:11-13)

Grace is a teacher. See that? "The grace of God has appeared... teaching us."

When you take in the Bible, you don't just receive information, you also receive power (Hebrews 4:12). By that power, energized by the Holy Spirit, God transforms your mind (Romans 12:2). Grace in your mind then seeps in and becomes grace in your emotions, instincts, relationships, and character. Grace is a teacher.

What lessons does grace teach? Let's break it down.

Denying ungodliness and worldly lusts... Grace never makes sin okay. God loves you too much to do that. Grace is a force of nature. Stronger than a lighting bolt, but as tender as a butterfly's wing, grace is God's power not to sin. Grace repels sin. Triumphs over it. Grace delivers you from the tyranny of all the self-destructive, people-hurting, dysfunctional tendencies buried deep inside your soul. Grace knocks all your nasty inner tyrants off their creepy thrones.

Why? Because God hates the things that break your heart. And God hates the stuff you do that breaks other people's hearts. Such is the love of God.

When you give yourself a hall-pass to sin, that pass has not been signed by Grace. When there is the slightest whisper in your mind that it doesn't matter, that whisper is not the voice of grace.

It is, rather, the voice of immature pride. It is the voice that has degraded God's grace into a bland leniency in which good and evil cease to matter.

When you spurn God's grace, you most often reap what you sow. You're stuck wandering the wilderness.

But when you embrace God's grace, and let it teach you, you will reap what God sows.

That's the deal I want.

Grace is a teacher. Keep graduating to higher experiences of grace.

Have you ever taken care of a puppy? Two unarguable facts about puppies: 1) They are the most adorable little creatures in the world. So cute. So sweet. It's hard not to love a puppy. 2) They are also the most annoying little creatures in the world. They're demanding. They make a mess. They create chaos. They smell. Puppies are a lot of work.

Puppies are beloved.

Puppies are a pain.

Pardon the analogy, but... Immature Christians are beloved. Immature Christians are a pain.

> And I, brethren, could not speak to you as to spiritual people but as to carnal, as to babes in Christ. I fed you with milk and not with solid food; for until now you were not able to receive it, and even now you are still not able. (1 Corinthians 3:1, 2)

This is my pastoral plea: please don't coast. Step away from the kiddie table. Join the main feast. Grow up to the point where God's matchless grace lends color to your attitudes, fragrance to your words, and tender strength to your actions.

4. Grow in Grace-victory (Romans 8:37).

> Yet in all these things we are more than conquerors through Him who loved us. (Romans 8:37)

More than conquerors.

This world is a theater of conflict. Angels and demons are watching. A great cloud of witnesses views the everyday battle that is your life. Spiritual warfare dogs every step of grace you take. What is the secret of victory?

It is not physical strength—the muscles you have trained, the endurance you have built up.

It is not mental attainment—your education and degrees and books you have read.

It is not social skill—that you are an extrovert and know how to work the room.

It is not your earthly wealth—for there is no victory in the spiritual realm that can be bought at any price.

No. In this great arena in which you stand, the triumph is nothing you produce by your own effort and strength.

What makes you strong, what makes you invincible, what makes the enemies of the cross snarl and snap is simply this:

The distinguishing mark of a mature Christian is unshakeable confidence in the love of Christ.

This is not as simple as it sounds.

And it is not a cliché, either.

You have set your emotions on the bedrock truth of "Jesus loves me, this I know, for the Bible tells me so."

Even though life's evidence argues against it, you believe, and so you act out of victory.

Let the giants hurl their insults.

Let the fortified cities ooze their quiet threats.

Let the impossibilities array themselves before you.

If you have taken the time to grow in grace, if you have refused the downward drag of complacency, if you have denied again and again the temptation to coast...

Then, and only then, can you wear the badge of honor... *MORE THAN A CONQUEROR.*

Defeat is not in the vocabulary of a mature child of God. You may be down, but you're never out.

You don't quit, because you know God loves you.

You don't give in, because you know God loves you.

You don't wilt, because you know God loves you.

You may be physically weak, small, clumsy, unimposing. Your speech may be broken. Your mind not what you wanted it to be. Your clothing out of date. Your looks a mess. And your health or finances a giant question mark.

But you are a living breathing receptacle of omnipotent grace from God, and that grace is mighty to deliver, mighty to save, mighty to conquer, and mighty to change the world.

God has set a land before you.

A place of blessing for you.

A place of glory for God.

You can coast, or you can be diligent to enter that land.

It's time to break through.

The only way to build a sustainable spirituality is through continual growth in grace. Otherwise, you always lurch from emergency to emergency, dependent and needy and sad.

You know what Cubs fans always say: "This year is our year."

As I'm writing this chapter in the fall of 2016, the Chicago Cubs are on a tear. They have made an incredible breakthrough. Historic. Breathtaking.

They boast the best record in baseball. They lead the league in pitching, in hitting, in wins. If ever the Cubs were poised win it all, this year is the year. As a lifetime Cubs fan, and the son of a Cubs fan (who was a minor league third baseman for the Cubs), I'm so excited I can't stand it.

I have to think that's how the angels feel when they watch you push back your chair at the kiddie table, and take those faltering steps toward the main feast—those faith-inspired steps toward a greater experience of grace than you ever thought possible.

The angels are cheering you on, and so am I. This is why God led you to pick up a book called *Grace Breakthrough*. This is your time. Your moment. Your season. This is the day you spit out the lie that once you're saved, you've arrived. Get unstuck. Grow in grace. And watch the giants fall.

Prayer

Lord,

Help me grow. I'm tired of the wandering. Tired of the wilderness. And tired of the kiddie table.

I believe you have showered an immense mountain of grace and blessing upon me—you blessed me with infinite treasures the day I was born again.

Now, I want to unwrap those grace-gifts. I want to experience them. I want to rise up to my inheritance. I don't want to walk away from acres of diamonds; I want to collect them, polish them, share them, and enjoy them. You have a Promised Land for me; deliver me from coasting in the wilderness.

Lord, I'm done with the kiddie table. I'm moving on up. I confess I can't do this by my own human strength. So you be my power, dear Lord. You be my strength. Let Christ be formed in me. Let your Holy Scriptures transform my mind. Let the Spirit wield the Sword of the Word with precision and power.

Make me a Caleb, and give me the mountain of grace, where I experience maximum grace from you, and you receive maximum glory from me.

Grow me up, I pray...

In Christ Alone,

Amen.

8

THE CONFIDENCE BREAKTHROUGH

Even the Christian must fear God. But it is another kind of fear. It is a fear rather of what might have been than of what is; it is a fear of what would come were we not in Christ. Without such fear there can be no true love; for love of the Saviour is proportioned to one's horror of that from which man has been saved. And how strong are the lives that are suffused with such a love! They are lives brave, not because the realities of life have been ignored, but because they have first been faced—lives that are founded upon the solid foundation of God's grace. May such lives be ours! –J. Gresham Machen

Fear knocked at the door. Faith answered. No one was there. –Author Unknown

And now, little children, abide in Him, that when He appears, we may have confidence and not be ashamed before Him at His coming. (1 John 2:28)

BIG LIE #8: FEAR KEEPS THE FAITHFUL FAITHFUL.

I STOOD THERE NAKED, in plain sight, head hanging down, mortified at the exposure. I faced humiliation as public as any I could imagine.

I am referring to my fear of Judgment Day.

This fear defined me for decades. It lurked in the shadows of everything I did.

The legalist mantra says, "Fear keeps the faithful faithful."

This worked for me. I feared final judgment. I feared loss of salvation. I feared God's disapproving frown. I feared the loss of status with my peers. I feared a remarkably unenthusiastic welcome into the heavenly realms. I feared failure. I feared I hadn't done it right in the first place, and wasn't really saved.

I had not made my gospel breakthrough, security breakthrough, identity breakthrough, or growth breakthrough.

I sat, stuck at the kiddie table.

Afraid of my own spiritual shadow.

There was a Bible verse I heard a thousand times as a kid growing up: "What a man does in secret, he will one day shout from the rooftops." This Scripture applied to Judgment Day, I was told. No doubt, it was the Death Star spawning my last-days' phobia.

It wasn't till I was much older that I made a startling discovery: *there's no such verse in the Bible.* Yes, some come close, but those words simply aren't biblical, not, at least, when it comes to the believer's final judgment.

Here's the closest I can find (Luke 12:3 and Matthew 12:36 are similar):

> Therefore do not fear them. For there is nothing covered that will not be revealed, and hidden that will not be known. Whatever I tell you in the dark, speak in the light; and what you hear in the ear, preach on the housetops. (Matthew 10:26,27)

Even if we apply this verse to the last judgment, it's still impossible to apply it to believers in Jesus. Otherwise, why would Jesus begin this saying with an exhortation not to fear?

This is a far cry from the frightening prospect that a naked little me would be shouting my secret sins from any rooftops throughout this life or the next. That discovery blew my mind. Like an addict's intervention, it changed the course of my life.

Shaking off fear's shackles became a huge part of my grace breakthrough. Here's how it happened.

The Guilt Trip

God used a book.

The setting was my cavernous high school gym. I was a senior at Chicago's massive Lane Technical High School, with a student body over 5,000 at the time. My gym coach was absent for the day, so we sat on hard wooden bleachers and used the hour as a study period.

I'd brought a book with me about Satan. Little did I know that the last quarter of that book shined a spotlight on guilt and the Cross of Christ. Growing up fundamentalist, as I did, I'd heard about the Cross a million times. But this time was different. It was the first time the death of Christ really clicked with me.

I suspect the reason is because the author framed the Cross within the topic of *guilt*—which happened to be my middle name. He explained how the devil's favorite tool was guilt. And how the devil screwed guilt into our backs as a handle to slam us around every once in a while.

Who told this guy about me?

My little high school heart was pounding. Pick-up basketball games echoed in the background. The smell of old gym shoes, rubber basketballs, and sweat permeated my senses. My world narrowed to a single point—words on a page illuminated by God's own Spirit.

There, the message of the Cross pierced my guilt and shame. I learned how my sins were lifted out of me that they might be transferred to Christ. I discovered how this transfer was comprehensive—encompassing every moral failure, past, present, and future. I read in wonder how the hammer of heaven pounded justice on the head of Christ, punishing him for my sins instead of punishing me.

And then I read about those wonderful words, IT IS FINISHED, the best words ever uttered on planet earth.

What was finished?

Everything that ever had to happen to bring my sorry soul to heaven *without the slightest whisper of my secret sin or shame.*

Suddenly, the cosmic plasma screen shattered in a million pieces.

Behind it, I saw the smiling face of God, my Father, who approved of me, and delighted in me more than words could tell.

Grace was real.

It was stronger, far more beautiful, and infinitely more effective than I'd ever thought it was before.

That day, God converted a gym into a sanctuary, as he settled a stupendous promise into my dysfunctional soul: "I, even I, am He who blots out your transgressions for My own sake; / And I will not remember your sins" (Isaiah 43:25).

What an epiphany!

I didn't need to fear the face of God for even one more nanosecond. He was eternally satisfied with me, just as I was.

I wanted to shout Hallelujah, but it felt weird in that setting.

Amazing grace shattered the lie that fear keeps the faithful faithful.

Assurance

Legalism's germs proliferate in the dank cellars of fear. They thrive in the moisture of an implacable deity—a God who simply can't be satisfied no matter how hard I try.

And yet, that day, God's sun shined down into the cellars of my heart, and my fear and shame withered away.

I do not count that day as the day of my salvation; I was saved before that, and I'm convinced it "took" the first time, and it "stuck" with me forever. God is that faithful.

I do, however, count that day as the day of my *assurance*. A major healing of much of my Grace Deficit Disorder. I have never seriously doubted my salvation since then, and I have never again stooped beneath the burdensome anticipation of a humiliating entrance to God's everlasting kingdom.

My guilt was gone, and with it the fear of judgment that fueled so much dysfunction in my life.

Breaking Bondage

For you did not receive the spirit of bondage again to fear, but you received the Spirit of adoption by whom we cry out, "Abba, Father." (Romans 8:15)

You're always running on one of two operating systems, legalism or grace. The spirit of bondage or the Spirit of adoption. You need to switch operating systems. Make the upgrade from legalism to grace. And as often as you fall into legalism you need to switch back again. I'm writing to motivate, hasten, enable, persuade, instruct, and celebrate that far-reaching switch.

To use a biblical term, you need to repent.

Biblical repentance is never a legalistic addition to the gospel. It is not the super-imposition of behavioral demands on the Walking Dead who are incapable of doing good. It does not consist of self-effort, self-will, or self-improvement.

Repentance is a radical change of mind—swapping out one worldview for another. Changing operating systems. Repentance is the work of God, by the Spirit of God, applying the Word of God to the child of God.

By it, you undergo a radical transformation of your whole way of looking at God, yourself, and your relationship with him. By it, you don't just change your mind, you overhaul it. God transforms your whole perspective on reality. It's time to swap out your old, tired, self-defeating worldview for God's holy, life-giving worldview.

Do you harbor the delusion you are inherently good enough for God? That if you are a sinner, you are only a sinner-lite? Repent.

Do you grade yourself on the curve? Do you justify yourself by comparing yourself to someone else—say a serial killer, or a "Bridezilla," or a serial-killing Bridezilla—and conclude you're just not that bad? Repent.

Have you swallowed "doctrines of demons" (1 Timothy 4:1), or have you suppressed the truth (Romans 1:18), elevating your own definitions of reality above the revealed declarations of God in the Scriptures? Repent.

Do you diminish the value and efficacy of the death of Christ on the Cross? Do you consider his work to be insufficient payment for your sin? Have you pursued the heartbreaking fallacy of self-atonement? Or denied you need atonement at all? Repent.

Are you chasing the happiness-butterfly through fields of activity the Bible calls sin? Or worldliness? Or foolishness? Or evil? Repent.

Do you honestly think you can reach God by climbing a latter of perfection? Do you have a solution for your sins apart from the finished work of Christ? Repent.

You can't just add the grace app to legalism's operating system and call it good. The whole thing will crash.

You need a whole new system, a grace-centric outlook on everything that matters.

You need a breakthrough.

Enter the most beautiful, coherent, logical, generous, all-encompassing Theory of Everything ever revealed in this cosmos or any other, humbly titled the Grace of God. There is nothing like it in the annals of world religion. Take history's smartest philosophers, the world's greatest religious leaders, and society's most noble women and men, throw them in a room together for a thousand years with the directive to concoct a religion, and the smartest people in the room would never come up with a system of grace. They'd come up with yet another variation on the same old theme: humans by human effort seeking to merit the approval of God.

Legalism owns the human instinct. That's because the Fall hardwired a lie into the soul. So Grace Deficit Disorder spreads like black mold beneath life's happy exterior.

You need to swap out the old system for the new one. The old covenant for the new covenant. Legalism for grace.

That swap is surgical. It's transformative. It's repentance.

Always More To Do

Legalism is "a spirit of bondage" which produces "fear." Under legalism, you can never be confident. You can never breathe easy. There's always another law to obey, sin to conquer, good work to perform.

Under the Old Testament system of sacrifices, there was no end to the blood flowing from the altar, as sacrifice followed upon sacrifice with no end in sight. You could never just sit down and rest in the abiding love of God. Fear of God. Fear of man. Fear of final judgment. Fear of exposure. Fear of people's opinions. Fear of the disapproving frown. Fear of outsider status. Fear of death, hell, the devil, and the corruptions ever ready to erupt from your own lunatic heart.

The legalistic operating system is built on this fear. Under legalism, fear keeps the faithful faithful.

Thank God for the Cross.

> And every priest stands ministering daily and offering repeatedly the same sacrifices, which can never take away sins. But this Man, after He had offered one sacrifice for sins forever, sat down at the right hand of God. (Hebrews 10:11,12)

Christ sat down because his work was complete. The age of bondage was over. Fear no longer owned mankind's instinct. A new age had been inaugurated.

You've received the Spirit of Adoption. You are no longer a slave, but a son or a daughter in the royal household of God.

Approach his throne with confidence. Come into his presence boldly. No cowering needed. No worries, no fears, and no jitters. Check your anxieties at the door. The angels salute you as you approach. Your clearance has been granted. Go to him. Go to him, and see a smile on his face that will melt your heart.

Under grace, the cry of your heart is no longer, "I'm scared," but "Abba, Father."

Dad, I'm home!

Everything is new.

Love keeps the faithful faithful. Gratitude. Confidence in future grace, more than enough for all your tomorrows. The great mystery of Christ in you.

Too bad, Satan.

Repentance is that eye-opening moment of realization in which you finally get what a dummy you've been, trying to work your way to God's favor instead of receiving a gift purchased by the blood of Christ.

It is the epiphany that your happiness lies in the hand of a Father who every day reaches toward you with a compassion that knows no bounds.

It is the discovery that life's anxieties are wasted in the presence of a throne of grace.

It is the stark realization of the stench rising up from your sins, and an urgent turning and returning unto the sufficiency of Christ's blood to wash you white as snow.

Repentance switches operating systems from legalism to grace.

It's epic.

Monumental.

It is the definition of a grace breakthrough.

By it, you switch from works to faith.

From earning it to receiving it.

From sweating over it to resting in it.

From earning a paycheck to accepting a gift.

From your efforts to Christ's efforts.

From your dedication to Christ's dedication.

From your sacrifice to Christ's sacrifice.

From shadow to substance.

From image to reality.

From religion to relationship.

From despair to hope.

From fear to faith.

From hell to heaven.

And from self to God.

You can't change your ways until you change your mind, and repentance is that change of mind.

If God is for you, who can be against you?

When God delivered me from my fear of judgment, he delivered me into a tremendous sense of peace. Whatever turmoil swirls around my life, whatever storms batter my ship of faith, I know my anchor holds, and one day, I'll sail into the haven of rest and step into that glorious realm where fears are no more.

Bill Giovannetti, step forward.

I'm here, Father.

Welcome home, Son.

Prayer

Loving Father,

If the death and resurrection of Jesus mean anything, they mean I don't have to fear your presence. You are as satisfied with me as you are with Christ—because you see me as one with him.

I hereby refuse to let *fear* drive my walk with you. Not fear, but love; not worry, but grace fuels me.

I read in your word that I should fear you, and I do—in the sense of honor, respect, and concern for your glory.

But by your grace, and because of Christ, I will not fear punishment from you, disapproval from you, or the removal of your presence or blessing. You wouldn't do those things to Christ, and since, I'm joined to him, you won't do those things to me.

I follow you out of trust, not fear. Out of love, not obligation. With joy, not drudgery. I declare my confidence that your grace will provide for all my tomorrows.

I repent of all beliefs that diminish your compassion and grace. I believe that you are who you say you are, and I am who you say I am.

I approach you with the easy confidence of a firstborn heir. And I say, with all boldness and faith, that I am blessed beyond words to be your child.

In Christ I pray,

Amen.

9

THE MISSION BREAKTHROUGH

We are Christ's ambassadors, and God is using us to speak to you. We urge you, as though Christ himself were here pleading with you, "Be reconciled to God!" (2 Corinthians 5:20, NLT)

Some want to live within the sound of church or chapel bell; / I want to run a rescue shop within a yard of hell. –C.T. Studd, 1800s

BIG LIE #9: SHARING CHRIST'S LOVE AND GRACE IN THE WORLD REQUIRES ME TO BE A FREAK.

WHEN YOU SEE A MOVIE, before the movie, you get twenty minutes of coming attractions. Previews. There are these blockbuster movies coming, and the previews entice the audience to want to be there. They always give you the most exciting scenes—action, adventure, romance—anything to hook the viewer into making sure they don't miss the movie.

There is a blockbuster coming soon; I'll bet you've heard of it.

The Producer is God the Father.

The Director is God the Holy Spirit.

The Leading Man is the Lord Jesus Christ.

You'll find adventure, drama, warfare, and romance all rolled into one.

It's called The Kingdom of God. In theology, it's called the Eternal State. It will be a world-wide release.

Actually bigger—it will play throughout the whole cosmos.

We believe Jesus is King, and one day, he will be seen as reigning King from shore to shore. Every eye will see him, and all the world will bow before King Jesus.

That is creation's big day. That is the coming coronation day for Jesus. That is heaven and earth's grandest production. There's nothing like the coming kingdom of Christ. It will be a blockbuster to end all blockbusters.

What a day that will be!

God has opened the theater of the cosmos and invited the whole race of humankind to come enjoy the show. This is his love. This is his amazing grace. "Whosoever will" may come.

God so passionately wants to fill the theater, that he has loaded the world with coming attractions. He is enticing the world, inviting the world, wooing the world, and calling the world.

What might those coming attractions be?

You.

Me.

All who bear the title Christian.

Why do you think you are still in this world?

Why do you think God didn't just beam you up the moment you believed in Jesus?

He left you on earth to serve as a coming attraction for heaven.

That's you. You bring a mini-slice of the kingdom of God to earth every single day. How? Not by following rules and laws. Not by legalism. Not by being weird, out of touch, or odd. Not by speaking a Christianized language of "anointing" and "the prophetic." And not by signs and wonders. You bring heaven to earth every single day by simply living a grace-filled life.

> For the kingdom of God is not eating and drinking, but righteousness and peace and joy in the Holy Spirit. (Romans 14:17)

Righteousness and peace and joy. That's how you bring heaven to earth.

Righteousness—the grace of God in your identity as it works out into a mature lifestyle, clean and delivered from habits that break your heart.

Peace—the grace of God in your relaxed mental attitude and freedom from debilitating fears.

Joy—the grace of God in your emotions, creating a heart at rest, confident in the love of Christ.

By the Holy Spirit—by God's own power, working out the life of Christ in you.

That's the way heaven shows up on earth. Not by you being odd. Not by you speaking a Christian-weirdo language. It's the devil's lie to say that only freakish Christians are effective witnesses.

Heaven shows up on earth whenever you radiate grace in your life. When you are strong, brave, and loving, and when you show faith when faith makes no sense. That's all the signs and wonders our broken world needs.

Heaven comes to earth when you see grace as your mission, from God, through God, and by God.

Your mission is to show forth the grace that will one day permeate the cosmos as salt permeates the sea. As a

142 | GRACE BREAKTHROUGH

result, men and women, boys and girls, will discover and embrace that same grace for themselves.

You are God's coming attraction.

Abiding in Christ

Sometimes it's hard to rest.

The Bible calls this "abiding in Christ."

You've worked hard all your life. Now it's time to simply abide.

I wrote this book to persuade you of a deeper, richer, fuller grace than you ever thought possible.

I've tried to put my finger on the anti-grace lies in your soul and call them out.

I've written to make you believe the great Scripture reality that you possess something absolutely fantastic. You've laid hold of something awesome. Actually, his grace laid hold of you. You have something better than you realize. If you have Jesus, you have a treasure beyond description. Any unbeliever who understood who you really are and what you really have would give anything to trade places with you.

You are the richest person you know. You are blessed. You have the very thing this worn out world needs most—what it craves most. You have the one thing that people around you every day are groping in darkness to find.

You've been made a full partner in the matchless grace of God.

You have discovered the grace that saves you, forgives you, and makes you God's own, in the Gospel Breakthrough.

You have rested in the grace that sets you on an unshakeable rock that cries out, "Once-saved, always-saved!" You've put to bed your doubts about your worth and acceptance, in the lap of your Security Breakthrough.

You have taken hold of a grace that rehabs your broken sense of self, peeling off years of painful labels, and showing forth your new self in all your beauty, through the Identity Breakthrough.

You have made the glorious shift from wrestling to clinging. From sweating, straining, cajoling, and conniving a blessing out of God to simply believing the best about him and from him in your Rest Breakthrough.

You have shrugged off the mantle of religious slavery and taken back the scepter of your life—rising up to your true dominion, and piloting your ship wherever you choose under the influence of Jesus Christ in your Freedom Breakthrough.

You have seized the grace that unleashes your true glory and saves you from a mediocre life of coasting your way to heaven, in the Growth Breakthrough.

And now, you're ready for the grace of the final breakthrough: the Mission Breakthrough.

For the rest of your days, you will find yourself on a mission to help people find and follow God.

Here's the great secret so few discover: this grace mission is the most natural thing in the world once you break through the legalism in your life.

Here are three ways that you join God's grace-mission in the world, and I'll bet you would never guess the first two.

Engaging Your Life-Mission

1. You engage your life-mission by experiencing maximum grace from God.

> To the praise of the glory of His grace, by which He has made us accepted in the Beloved. (Ephesians 1:6)

Your mission to the world can only thrive in the overflow of God's grace in your life. "My cup runneth over," King David said (Psalm 23:5, KJV).

There's that tremendous phrase in Ephesians 1:6: "the glory of his grace."

When I was a young pastor, I led a Bible study for our church's youth leaders. We studied through Ephesians, and I came to this verse and this phrase. It stumped me. What did it mean? What was "the glory of his grace"?

So I dug into the phrase. I saw how some modern translations make it say: "his glorious grace." That's actually a legit translation, but I don't think it's the best.

The more I studied, the more it hit me what this meant: *the glory that flows from the source of his grace.* [For our Greek-scholar friends, let's call this a genitive of source.]

The source of God's glory is his grace.

That hit me like a lightning bolt. It turned everything around for me.

Do you realize what that means? It probably means the opposite of what you've always thought.

The great goal of all creation is to glorify God. To bring honor and praise to his name. God made you for his glory. His glory is your Prime Directive in time and eternity.

Well, if the great purpose for your life's existence is to glorify God, it follows that you should be crystal clear about how that is done.

How does a person glorify God? We should have a ready answer.

Many Christians do have an answer, but most of them aren't just wrong, they're backwards. They're one hundred eighty degrees out of phase with God's truth.

So they wind up serving the wrong mission.

If I ask Christians how to glorify God, most will answer in terms of behavior: Do good works. Let your light shine. Be a good person. Live up to your high calling. Sacrifice your comfortable Christian life and go do something radical for Jesus.

Those are all good things, but I would assert that not one of them unlocks the secret of maximizing the glory of God.

It was when I studied this verse in Ephesians, and found so many other Scriptures that make the same connection, I was blown away. It was a breakthrough, and it redefined my mission in life.

His glory flows from the source of his grace.

His grace means that which he does for me, not what I do for him.

Therefore, his glory flows from the source of all that he does for me, not from what I do for him.

Let me put it this way: to speak of "the glory of his grace" is to say that *God is glorified, not by what you do for him, but by what he does for you.*

The glory of God is his grace.

If there is going to be a shining light in your neighborhood, in your workplace, in your classroom, in your corporate boardroom, in your prison ward, or in your hospital—if there is going to be a shining light of the gospel of Jesus Christ—then that light will shine most brightly in the life of a person who consciously experiences a God-blessed life.

When you can testify that your cup runs over, your lost friends will pay attention.

The Mission Breakthrough does not require you to be weird, the devil's lie notwithstanding. Nor does it require you to turn your back on God's blessing in your life.

I am worn out by rousing calls to hyper-activity within the church in the name of glorifying God. Pastors, books, conferences, and seminars routinely summon God's weary people to ever more activity and busy-ness and sacrifice and service. Don't get me wrong; those are good things, in their place.

But unless those good things live in the overflow of grace, they are not God things.

Grace Deficit Disorder already runs at epidemic levels in the church. Even so, along comes preacher after preacher to flog God's people into doing ever more for Jesus.

That hurts the mission more than helps it.

Why?

Because they are not resting in the grace of God.

Because they are not abiding in the fellowship of Christ.

Because they are not rehabbing their sense of identity in Christ.

Because they are not tapping into their riches in Christ.

Because they are not leaning on Jesus, because they hardly know who he is or what he has done.

They are not abiding in Christ, so whatever fruit the sweat of their brow produces only sours in the mouths of those who taste it.

If they are a "coming attraction," it's only for a movie no one wants to see.

I want nothing more than to see true revival in our day. I want to see men and women, boys and girls, be carried across that chasm from death to life. I long and pray for that day when you can lead your friend to Christ, your dying father or mother to Christ, your neighbor or fellow student to Christ.

I can't wait for you to join with God in the grand mission of grace, telling the story of Jesus in ever expanding circles and around the world.

But never forget: the glory of God is his grace—what he does for you, in you, by you, and through you. God's work, God's power, God's gift.

Paul said, "To this end I also labor, striving according to His working which works in me mightily" (Colossians 1:29). Just whose *works* are in view here?

What that means for us is simple: the calling card for your testimony is the depth of your experience of grace.

Why should anyone listen to you when you speak of Christ?

Because you have credibility born of a mature walk in grace.

You have suffered loss, and grace has been your comfort.

You have not known which way to turn, and grace has been your guide.

You have shed tears and felt pain, and grace has met your need and gone beyond.

You have chosen the path of honor—the ethical path, the righteous path, the life-giving path—even though it cost you.

You have overcome insurmountable temptations, reconciled destroyed relationships, risen above long-term addictions, and broken through clouds of despair.

Every careworn crease written across your smiling face is yet another testimony to the all-sufficient grace of Almighty God.

So when you speak, people listen. Because the blessing of God in your life is utterly beyond argument.

Grace makes your whole life a coming attraction for the gospel.

God's glory shines brightly through you because God's grace has settled deeply in you.

The glory of grace is your calling card, and when you speak of Jesus, the look of long experience silences every critic. You've proven the gospel's worth through thick and thin.

The way you join God's grace-mission on planet earth starts when you experience maximum grace from him. That's probably not what you expected.

Here's another unexpected mission-minded twist:

2. You engage your life-mission by just being yourself.

> But now God has set the members, each one of them,
> in the body just as He pleased. (1 Corinthians 12:18)

I started my pastoral ministry as a youth pastor, and after that I planted a church in Chicago. Windy City Community Church; it's still going strong. I pastored Windy City for sixteen years.

As a young, novice, senior pastor, I had some growing to do. Right at that time, there was a very big church in the Chicago suburbs that took off like a rocket. You might have heard of Willow Creek Community Church and pastor Bill Hybels.

I attended Bill Hybels' youth group when I was a kid and I heard him speak many times. He has a remarkable ability to get under your skin.

His church was growing by leaps and bounds, and he had pioneered a certain kind of preaching. He called it seeker-sensitive preaching. Hybels spoke mainly to unchurched people.

So I figured I'd copy him. I started preaching like him. I wanted to be just like him.

It was a disaster. I wasn't happy. My church wasn't thriving. And I made a discovery:

I can't be Bill Hybels, and Bill Hybels can't be Bill Giovannetti. So I decided to be Bill Giovannetti and teach the Bible the way I teach the Bible. I'll just be myself.

I've never looked back.

That was the real me.

God called me to be a pastor and to preach the Word of Grace from a pulpit. He might not have called you to that. That does not make you a second-rate disciple. Nor does it make me better than anybody else.

A humble mom struggling with her kid's math homework helps the mission of God just as much as a preacher preaching to thousands. Just be yourself.

A dad or mom working on cars to put food on the family's table is contributing to the mission of grace, just by their everyday faith.

You do not need to sell all your possessions. Just be yourself. Your redeemed best self. Then, follow your heart.

You do not need to go to Africa or an impoverished nation. Just be yourself.

You do not need to be radical. You do not need crazy love or crazy anything. You do not need to follow in some super-pastor's footsteps. You do not need to be a weird Jesus-clone.

You just need to be your truest, most authentic self in your place, in your time, whatever that looks like, even if it's frazzled and frumpy and kind of chaotic. As long as grace is there, your testimony has all the power it needs.

Grace isn't always clean cut and tidy.

Sometimes, grace is messy.

Whether you are a janitor pushing a broom, or a CEO in a boardroom, do what you do by God's grace, and for his glory, and someway, somehow, God will weave that into a great mission of helping people find and follow God.

You are a unique creation of God. You don't have to be like anyone else. You don't have to try to be like anybody else.

Grace cries out, *Just be yourself.*

Because you will come across as real. You will be natural. You will be doing what you were created to do. When you speak of Christ, you won't come across as reading from a script or as pitching a sale.

Your whole life offers a coming attraction of heaven, and people want what you have.

You shine forth as a normal person — relatively, hopefully — who can bear witness that Jesus is as alive in small apartments as he is in big mansions. He is equally mighty to save high school dropouts and college professors. He loves blue-collar workers and unemployed teachers, and he can save and bless poor people, rich people, and middle class people without breaking a sweat.

It's legalism that makes you live by other people's rules.

It's legalism that traps you in past trauma and pain and loss.

It's legalism that says who you are can never be enough.

It's legalism that makes you try to be somebody you're not.

It's legalism that says only super-Christians are good Christians.

We are talking about the mission of bringing the Gospel of Grace to a lost and dying world.

We are talking about a Mission Breakthrough—a mission to serve up heaping platters of saving grace into your spiritually starving world.

Why is it a breakthrough?

Because legalism transmogrifies being on mission for God into a penance. Legalism flogs people for not being super-Christians. Look at the best selling books. Listen to the biggest conferences. You hear so little of Christ and his cross. So little of this fountainhead of all grace. The blood-accented language of Calvary is all but missing. Christianity is not preached as the grace of Christ in us. No. Instead this first wonder of the world has mutated into a wearisome treadmill of tasks, ministries, duties, obligations, and burdens no mortal can bear.

We've created a weird sub-culture in the church, and it's freakishly off-putting to the unsaved world.

And to God, though his love never even flickers.

Where is the preaching of the Cross? We hear so little of the saving work of Christ, and the sanctifying work of the Holy Spirit. So little of God's grace and so much of our duty.

Instead there's too much clichéd preaching, too much application, to shallow an approach to Scripture, too little of the doctrines of grace, and hardly any Calvary at all.

There's something about church people that makes us love getting rebuked. We flock to the speakers who wave the giant foam finger of shame. All too often, we make their shame-based books bestsellers. It's insane. It's Grace Deficit Disorder on steroids.

Legalism turns being on mission for God into a form of grueling self-sacrifice.

But grace turns that mission into self-expression. Do you know why? Because grace rehabs your identity first. It rehabs your sense of *self*. That means when you express your true self—your identity in Christ— something like this will happen:

> Thus says the LORD of hosts: "In those days ten men from every language of the nations shall grasp the sleeve of a Jewish man, saying, 'Let us go with you, for we have heard that God is with you.'" (Zechariah 8:23)

People will say, *If you're a coming attraction, I really want to see the show.*

You will say, *That's great, and guess what! Your admission is paid.*

Doesn't it make sense that a mission to proclaim grace would employ methods that manifest grace?

Here is one more way to engage your life-mission here on planet earth:

3. Join your life to a church that relentlessly proclaims Christ, crucified, risen, and coming again.

Jesus said, "I will build My church, and the gates of Hell shall not prevail against it" (Matthew 16:18).

There's a war going on. Victory is assured. Christ guaranteed it. Souls are at stake. Eternal souls.

Grace wins in the end. Grace, not leniency. Grace, not a love so wimpy it doesn't mean anything. Grace wins—that perfect melding of blistering holiness and self-giving love that flows from the heart of God through an old rugged cross to a lost and dying world.

Grace wins.

Some people are saved by this grace. Some people are lost by resisting it. Some people go to heaven. Some people go to hell. It's that simple and it's that stark.

Grace is the beautiful force in God's heart that desires all people everywhere to come to Jesus as Savior.

And when Christ moved into you, he brought that passion with him. Engaging the mission is the most natural thing for the person who has grown in grace.

Jesus said he will be the one to build his church. That's *his* work. Our task is to come alongside, and let him live through us, speak through us, and shine through us.

"Church" happens when Christ-filled people assemble for worship and equipping in the Word, and then scatter to bring the gospel of Christ to a needy world.

So Jesus invites you to partner with his people in the great mission of helping people find and follow God.

Through deeds of kindness.

Through self-giving love.

Through hands of help for those in need.

Through embracing life's last in line.

Through gentleness toward a wounded world.

Through representing Christ in boardrooms and classrooms.

Through standing against evil.

But above all else, through speaking the words of the gospel of grace, for "how shall they believe in him of whom they have not heard?" (Romans 10:14).

I've been around the church block enough times to know I would never partner with a church where lost people weren't routinely being saved. It's just my thing, I guess.

I often hear "concerns" over churches that are too big, too loud, too contemporary, or too "institutional."

Might I lovingly suggest we be finished with those complaints?

So what, if a church is loud or big or small or sedate? If they're getting people saved, and helping those people become rooted and grounded in grace, I'm a fan. No matter how loud or quiet, organized or disorganized, contemporary or traditional they may be. Hopefully, those churches *should* be getting bigger or at least growing by conversion. What do you want them to do? Shut the doors and stop letting lost people in? Whisper about the salvation miracles they see? Settle for the people they already have and coast their way to glory?

No way!

Shout it to the rooftops: GOD STILL SAVES! WE SEE IT WITH OUR OWN EYES!

There is no sign so grand or wonder so glorious as a sinful soul stepping across salvation's threshold by grace through faith in the Savior.

When grace flows through a church, the church bleeds for lost people, hurting people, rich and poor people, all people.

Big churches, and small churches—God loves them all. And all can accomplish their mission as long as lost people are routinely saved and evangelism isn't buried in an avalanche of complacency masquerading as "fellowship."

Being right about grace isn't about winning a point, it's about winning the lost.

Why the Mission Breakthrough?

Why is it so important for us to make this grace-based mission breakthrough?

Because we care about people—grace has made us tender-hearted.

Because we know life without Christ is harder than it needs to be and eternity without him is unspeakably sad—grace has birthed a deep concern in our hearts.

Because we want everyone to find the treasure we found when we found Jesus—grace gave us a discovery that we can't hold in.

Because we're excited to see people we care about be transformed by the love of God—grace makes us passionate for the gospel.

Because Christ's own love has ignited a fire in our bellies and we can't keep quiet (Romans 5:5)—grace is the best news we've ever heard and we just can't help ourselves.

Because the grace of God has become our theme... and shall be till we die.

I pray you break through every legalism and bondage and fear.

I pray you rise above the dark forces of defeat and complacency.

I pray you fill your mind with the Cross of Christ, and the beauty of the Savior, and the powers of resurrection-love, and the wonders of divine grace.

I pray grace works mighty miracles in you as God rehabs your sense of self, and you begin to live out of that new self.

I pray that you, in your place for such a time as this, will become a beautiful, appealing, and irresistible preview of everlasting wonders to come.

Prayer

Precious Lord,

How I thank you for the people who told me about Jesus and your matchless grace in him. Thank you for those who loved me, prayed for me, answered my questions, taught me, and put up with me while I kicked and fought against grace.

For the Cross of Christ—the fountain of all grace—I give you endless praise.

For whatever grace breakthroughs I have made, I give you all the glory.

For whatever guilt and shame I have been enabled to release at the foot of the Cross, I humbly bless your name.

And now Lord, I want to join the ranks of witnesses who proclaim a grace that still saves the lost. I want my life to be a coming attraction for heaven—a living, breathing proclamation of the matchless grace of Christ.

Equip me, Lord, to lead people to Christ.

Use me in the grand adventure of helping lost people receive your great salvation.

I will shine your grace-energized light. I will be my grace-filled self. I will speak the grace-only gospel.

I long to tell the old, old story of Jesus and his love. I long to live it too.

And I pray for the day when grace breaks through the hardest hearts I know, to shine the light of the glorious gospel to those who do not believe.

In Christ I pray,

Amen.

10

TOP TEN GRACE BREAKTHROUGHS IN THE BIBLE

But as it is written: "Eye has not seen, nor ear heard, Nor have entered into the heart of man The things which God has prepared for those who love Him." (1 Corinthians 2:9)

I saw myself standing outside a house looking in on a tremendous party with laughter and joy. The Lord tracked me down and found me. I was surprised by grace. I became an avid Bible reader and my initial doubts soon evaporated in the atmosphere of solid Bible exposition at the Christian Union. -J.I. Packer

BIG LIE #10: NOW THAT I'VE LEARNED ABOUT GRACE, I CAN MOVE ON TO SOMETHING ELSE.

NOBODY EVER GRADUATES out of Christ's school of grace. Grace is a bottomless ocean of blessing and joy. An endless supply. A relationship with our infinite God. You will never plumb its depths. You will never exhaust its potential. Heaven will be the ever-expanding discovery of the depths of infinite grace: "that in the ages to come He might show the exceeding riches of His grace in His kindness toward us in Christ Jesus" (Ephesians 2:7).

In the spirit of always leaving room for more, let's look at ten people in the Bible who had another grace-breakthrough to enjoy.

10. Moses

Grace Deficit Disorder: I am not eloquent enough to persuade Pharaoh to let God's people go.

Grace Breakthrough: "Now therefore, go, and I will be with your mouth and teach you what you shall say." (Exodus 4:12)

In the dramatic encounter between God and Moses at the burning bush, nothing screams Grace Deficit Disorder like Moses arguing his inadequacy to God. I can't do what you're telling me to do, because I'm such a mess.

Yet there's a beautiful promise from God waiting for him here. God tells a man who can't imagine saying a single word to Pharaoh, "I will be with your mouth."

With your mouth.

I imagine that if Moses doubted his elbows, God would promise to be with his elbows.

Or his face. His hairline. His I.Q. His muscles. His complexion. Waistline. Pinky toes. Wallet. Or with any other inadequacy he felt.

You could say that Moses started out as a reluctant recipient of grace. I'm glad the power lies in God's grace, not in our faith. That's why even shaky, weak, fickle, mustard-seed faith wins the day.

Moses stuck to script, "Let my people go."

God was with his mouth.

And a nation was reborn.

When grace breaks through, slaves go free—no matter what person, experience, emotion, addiction, delusion, institution, or power has held them in chains. That's the lesson of Moses and his grace breakthrough.

9. Jonah

Grace Deficit Disorder: I am so ticked off that God saved those nasty people of Nineveh that I wish I could die.

Grace Breakthrough: Jonah, you're more worried about a dying plant than about 120,000 spiritually dying people who don't know their spiritual right hand from their spiritual left.

But the Lord said, "You have been concerned about this vine, though you did not tend it or make it grow. It sprang up overnight and died overnight. But Nineveh has more than a hundred and twenty thousand people who cannot tell their right hand from their left, and many cattle as well. Should I not be concerned about that great city?" (Jonah 4:10, 11, NIV)

Jonah's little hissy fit revealed a chaotic vacuum where his grace should be. As a prophet of God, he should have jumped for joy over the prospect of another nation found by the grace of God.

But no. An ultra-reluctant Jonah preached. The Assyrians embraced God's grace—from the king on down. And Jonah got so ticked off he wanted to die.

He'd rather preach to the choir back at home, I guess. Not that there's anything wrong with that—I've seen the choir, and they need preaching!

But Jesus told us, "Go into all the world and preach the gospel to every creature" (Matthew 16:15). There's this outward, expansive, go-get-em force to grace-filled Christianity.

Christians can be very loving to one another, yet very alienating to lost people around them — and never even know it. And that is the sickest disease a church can have.

Jonah plopped down in the hot sun to whine over Nineveh's conversion by the gospel of grace.

God graciously shaded him with a plant.

Later the plant died.

Jonah's whining kicked into overdrive.

So God gave him a grace-kick in the seat of the pants. A breakthrough that never broke through.

Listen Mr. Prophet Holy Man... you care more about the temporal death of that stupid plant than about the eternal death of a 120,000 people. Look at yourself. Don't you see that something's wrong?

Paul said, "For the love of Christ compels us..." (2 Corinthians 5:14). When the theology of Christ's love grips the psychology of your heart, grace takes root and you will naturally ache for people who have yet to find the treasure you found when you found Christ.

8. Mephibosheth

Grace Deficit Disorder: Then he bowed himself, and said, "What is your servant, that you should look upon such a dead dog as I?" (2 Samuel 9:8)

Grace Breakthrough: "As for Mephibosheth," said the king, "he shall eat at my table like one of the king's sons." (2 Samuel 9:11)

Life is not easy for those with any kind of disability, and it was doubly hard in the ancient world. Sadly, many cultures blamed the victim—*you must be a very bad person for God/the gods to make you suffer like that* (see John 9:2). This still happens today. In addition to his mouthful of a name, Mephibosheth had three strikes against him.

Strike One: the Bible says "...And he was lame in both his feet" (2 Samuel 9:13). Like I said, a difficult thing at any time, and even more so in ancient days. He became disabled during infancy, when his well-meaning nurse fell on him while fleeing a palace coup.

Compare his physical disability to the spiritual disability of a grace-starved heart.

Strike Two: he was the heir of a dead king, the last of a deposed dynasty. In an age when the new king wiped out the old king's dynasty, Mephibosheth found himself in permanent exile, far from a throne he would never enjoy.

Compare this to the exile of a graceless soul from its birthright as a child of heaven's King.

Strike Three: Mephibosheth was now groveling on the floor before King David, having been summoned from the barren land of his exile. At this point, Mephibosheth labeled himself a "dead dog" (2 Samuel 9:8).

Compare this to a life stuck in the badlands of brokenness and sin.

Strike three, Mephibosheth. You're out!

We're all out, too. By nature and practice, we're all a bunch of dead dogs too—though some might be too proud to admit it.

Thank you, God, for grace.

In a stunning reversal, King David comforts Mephibosheth and tells him to quit groveling. David restores his dignity, restores his wealth, gives him the best servants in town, and sets him in the nicest seat at the royal table, not just for one meal, but for a lifetime.

Scripture bends over backwards to identify this story as an illustration of a grace breakthrough. The whole thing begins when King David asks if there is any survivor of the house of King Saul that he might show "the grace [Heb.: *hesed*] of God."

If you want to know what a grace breakthrough looks like, take a look at bent-over Mephibosheth, pounding down gourmet lasagna at the sumptuous table of the king.

When you see yourself as blessed better than you deserve, you've made Mephibosheth's grace breakthrough.

7. David

Grace Deficit Disorder: "Hey God, my house is better than your house, so I will build a house for you! Yes!" [The prophet Nathan: "You Go David!"]

Grace Breakthrough: "Hey David, did I ever ask you to build a house for me? Here's the basic idea of your whole crazy life: I WILL BUILD A HOUSE FOR YOU." [The prophet Nathan: "I guess I got the whole thing backwards."]

> Then King David went in and sat before the LORD; and he said: "Who am I, O LORD God? And what is my house, that You have brought me this far?" (1 Chronicles 17:16)

People don't just mess up grace a little bit; they invert it, turn it on its head, and get it exactly backwards.

Case in point, noble king David.

In a fit of personal piety, David proposed a project to the prophet *du jour*. "God's house is so ordinary and plain compared to mine. I will build God an ultra-fabulous house, a temple to beat all temples! Yes, I will do this for my God! Amen."

Even without a swelling orchestral background, one can feel the grandeur of this moment. After all, isn't most preaching and writing geared to get Christians to do stuff for God? Isn't that the whole ball game?

The prophet Nathan thought so. He put the divine stamp of approval on David's ambitious plan. Believe me, most preachers would. Heck, I would too. If anybody in my church proposed a building program and wanted to pay for it for the glory of God, there's no way I'd turn them down.

Which only goes to show how deeply mired we all are in Grace Deficit Disorder.

Fact: Christianity is not about what you do for God.

Fact: Christianity is about what God has done, is doing, and will do for you through and because of Jesus Christ.

Let's use arrows to point which way life's blessings flow. When God blesses us, arrows point down from heaven to earth. When we bless God, arrows point up, from us earthlings to God. (More on this in my book, *Grace Intervention*, Barbour Publishing, 2014).

David's plan to build a house for God was a gigantic arrow pointing up. Because everybody knows a homeless God isn't worth following.

Wait a minute.

What if God isn't homeless after all? What if, spiritually speaking, we're the homeless ones?

So that night, God flipped David's (and Nathan's) arrows over. Notice this exact reversal in this little exchange:

> Now then, tell my servant David, "This is what the LORD Almighty says: I took you from the pasture and from following the flock, to be ruler over my people Israel [arrow down]. I have been with you wherever you have gone [arrow down], and I have cut off all your enemies from before you [arrow down]. Now I will make your name like the names of the greatest men of the earth [arrow down]. And I will provide a place for my people Israel and will plant them so that they can have a home of their own and no longer be disturbed [arrow down]. Wicked people will not oppress them any more, as they did at the beginning and have done ever since the time I appointed leaders over my people Israel [arrow down]. I will also subdue all your enemies [arrow down]. I declare to you that the LORD will build a house for you [massive arrow down]..." (1 Chronicles 17:7-10, NIV)

Grace made a breakthrough. David sat stunned. He said the only thing a rational person would say when they realize how blessed they are by the grace of God: "Who am I?"

Who am I, that you should be this good to me?

Who am I, that you should know my name?

Who am I, that I should be so utterly forgiven?

Who am I, that you should pay the freight to save me, secure me, grow me, employ me, and carry me safely all the way to my heavenly home?

Who am I, that you should build a house of grace for me?

He was the richest, most powerful, most successful one-percenter on earth, and yet he asked, "Who am I?"

Arrow reversal maneuver complete. Another grace breakthrough.

I can't leave this story without pointing out the weirdly awesome verse that ends it:

> "And yet this was insignificant in Your eyes, O Lord GOD, for You have spoken also of the house of Your servant concerning the distant future. And this is the custom of man, O Lord GOD." (2 Samuel 7:19, NAS95)

He experienced the mother of all grace breakthroughs and announced, "And this is the custom of man."

It seems dull, but it's actually thrilling, once you get it.

The various Bible translations are all over the map on this verse (check it out for yourself). Some translations make it a question; others make it a statement. The phrase is variously translated "manner of man" (NKJV), "usual way of dealing with man" (NIV), "custom of man" (NASB), or "do you deal with everyone this way?"(NLT).

Let's break it down.

It's a simple sentence with only three Hebrew words, two of which you probably know. For real.

This... it's the Hebrew word *zoat,* which rhymes with boat.

Custom... it's the Hebrew word *torah,* which normally is translated *law.* It means a fundamental principle. An operating system. A root-level reality. I'll bet you already knew this Hebrew word.

Man... it's the Hebrew word *adam,* which can either be the name of our Great-Great-etc. Grandpa or, as in this case, a word meaning *mankind.* I'll bet you knew this Hebrew word too.

Putting it all together, we get: "This [is] the law of mankind."

What is the law of mankind?

Arrows pointing down.

Grace.

Grace is the law of mankind. The most fundamental reality. The bedrock truth. The only operating system that will never crash.

Grace.

God just reversed David's arrows, and David realized it's always and forever going to stay that way. So he cried out, "Grace is the fundamental operating system for all mankind!" It's the root level reality. Dig through all the layers of everything, and when you hit bedrock, you'll see God's universe is made of solid, 24,000,000 karat grace.

That's the lesson of David's breakthrough.

Grace is the law of mankind.

There it is, this precious declaration, tucked into the middle of the Old Testament for all to see, and obscured by translators who missed the point.

I guess it's too simple.

I guess their arrows were stuck pointing up.

Thank God for grace breakthroughs!

6. Naomi

Grace Deficit Disorder: "Woe is me. God is against me. Call me Bitterness Personified" (author's paraphrase). "But she said to them, "Do not call me Naomi; call me Mara, for the Almighty has dealt very bitterly with me." (Ruth 1:20)

Grace Breakthrough: "And may he be to you a restorer of life and a nourisher of your old age; for your daughter-in-law, who loves you, who is better to you than seven sons, has borne him." (Ruth 4:15)

This fallen world is a morally corrupt Pain Machine. Losses happen. Death overtakes all. Sin and evil crush the spirit. Bad people do bad things. Other people's craziness makes life difficult. Natural disasters add their misery.

It's not all bad, and there is plenty of good in the world, thanks to God's creative heart, and the tarnished relics of the image of God still within us. Yes, there's a lot of good in the world.

But all too many times, evil triumphs. This big old world is a morally corrupt Pain Machine.

And we're all stuck inside it. Case in point: Naomi. You're not even half a chapter into the Book of Ruth before she has faced famine, voluntary exile, the death of her husband, single parenthood, the death of Son

One, and the death of Son Two. You can add poverty to the mix. And loneliness amidst a people who don't even speak her own mother tongue.

She blames God for this feast of misery. "The Almighty has dealt very bitterly with me."

But is she right? Is her suffering God's fault?

In this brilliantly crafted, utterly captivating work of theology called The Book of Ruth, the author will insist the answer is no. Naomi is not right.

And neither are you when you blame God for the suffering in your life and your world.

God is not the author of evil. Never has been, never will be (James 1:13; Habakkuk 1:13).

It's the Pain Machine. When sin galloped into this world—by satanic instigation coupled with human invitation—death, disease, heartbreak, and pain came riding on its back.

In this world, you will have tough times. But don't give up hope: Christ has overcome the world (John 16:33).

Throughout the story of Ruth, the various characters serve up various opinions about God. Their opinions, however, may be distorted, like Naomi's.

That's from the *characters* in the story.

Then, along comes the *Narrator* of the story to serve up a reality check. Only twice, the unnamed Narrator speaks of God, once at the beginning, and once at the end.

At the beginning, the Narrator says: "For the Lord had visited his people in giving them bread" (Ruth 1:6). The Hebrew verb is *nathan* and it is translated *give*. This "giving" reverses the famine that started the whole mess.

At the end, the Narrator says: "The Lord gave [Ruth] conception, and she bore a son" (Ruth 4:13). Same verb. This "giving" reverses the death that accelerated the whole mess.

In a beautifully crafted, God-inspired work like Ruth, this kind of repetition is not by accident. It's a purposeful verbal frame around Naomi's grace breakthrough.

Maybe God is not the "taker" in the story of your life. Maybe he's the "giver." The ultimate giver. The all-time, undisputed, undefeated Champion Giver.

When the Pain Machine has chewed you up for a while, it's difficult to see the grace. But you must. Search for it. Hunt for it. Dig it out. Because it's there. Grace is always there for you, because God is always there for you. In Christ, he's not against you. He's for you. Not even the darkest night can block his grace from shining down on you.

God has blessings in the pipeline coming your way. Don't give up hope. Don't blame God for your heartbreaks, either. He's working to mend you, strengthen you, shield you, and enable you to rise above the power of the Pain Machine.

The lesson of Naomi's breakthrough is that one day, God's giant Grace Machine will finish chewing up the Pain Machine, and will spit it out. Until then, find the grace. And don't turn bitter against God.

5. Esther

Grace Deficit Disorder: My people have a huge problem—a Hitler-like thug named Haman—and I have to solve it.

Grace Breakthrough: Problem solved in Esther 6, and she isn't even in the room. Haman's downfall begins without one bit of help from Esther.

One of the ugly spin-offs of the giant Pain Machine is a force of nature called Other People's Craziness (OPC). Let's all admit we've brought down a fair share of misery on our own heads. Our own dumb choices and weak character account for much of the stress in our lives.

True enough?

It's also true, however, that a lot of other people have thrown their toxic ingredients into the stew of who I am. Bullies. Mean girls. Exploiters. Abusers. Criminals. Politicians. Corporate elites. Bureaucrats. The DMV. I swim in an ocean of other people's craziness.[1]

In the book of Esther, we see two of God's best people navigate the treacherous waters of the insane Persian court. Esther, guided by Uncle Mordecai, must deal with off-the-charts craziness ranging from sexual exploitation to a threatened holocaust of the entire race of the Jews.

Through no choice of her own, only Esther is in a position to save the day. But she can't. Haman has her

---

[1] See my forthcoming lifestyle commentary on Esther, *Mindgames: Rising Above Other People's Craziness* (Endurant Press, 2017) to dig into this topic.

cornered. He has wrapped the wimpy king around his little finger. The day of death draws near. Esther can do nothing about it but call the people to fast and pray.

Other People's Craziness, it seems, is about to triumph once again. It seems this way all too often. We're yanked around by the whims of life's power-brokers, and they're either nuts or evil or both. We so often find ourselves, like Esther, hunkered down, waiting for the axe to fall.

With remorseless understatement, the Author of Esther initiates the downfall of Haman—and of the diabolical plot he hatched—in a scene where Esther isn't even in the room. You can see for yourself in Esther chapter six. Even the wife of powerful Haman will soon pat him on the head and say, "It's been nice, Babe, but you're doomed" (paraphrase of Esther 6:13).

Have you ever had a problem that solved itself? Those are the moments when grace breaks through. God works while you rest. Or fret or worry or complain. God intervenes. God acts. You watch. Hopefully, you say thank you. Eventually.

Esther's breakthrough proves that God can make impossible problems evaporate like the morning fog. Grace unties the tightest knots other people's craziness creates. Grace makes a way around other people's evil. Grace parts the raging sea, and bids you cross on dry ground. Grace even cleans the mess of your own dumb choices.

4. The Adulterous Woman

Grace Deficit Disorder: They said to Him, "Teacher, this woman was caught in adultery, in the very act. Now Moses, in the law, commanded us that such should be stoned. But what do You say?" (John 8:4, 5)

Grace Breakthrough: When Jesus had raised Himself up and saw no one but the woman, He said to her, "Woman, where are those accusers of yours? Has no one condemned you?" She said, "No one, Lord." And Jesus said to her, "Neither do I condemn you; go and sin no more." (John 8:10, 11)

Busted.

Guilty.

There she was, lying on the ground. Covering her head, her face, trying to cover her half naked body and her shame. Feeling the leering eyes of her accusers. Dreading the strike of the first stone fired to kill her.

An adulteress. Caught in the act, and now exposed for all to see. Under the harsh law of moral rectitude, she deserved death. All sin does, ultimately. Now she's being used to make a point. To trap Jesus. He must either be harsh, and condemn her to die, or be lenient, and violate the Law of Moses in the process.

Trapped!

At least the religious lawyers thought so.

But Jesus is never trapped. Neither is his grace. Grace always sees a third way. Another option. A way to break through.

"Let him who is without sin among you cast the first stone."

Is the law of moral rectitude honored? Yes.

Is the kindness and love of God's heart honored? Yes.

Welcome to this amazing thing called grace.

Jesus makes two statements to this adulterous woman. They are important, not only for their content, but also for their order.

First he says, "Neither do I condemn you."

Second he says, "Go and sin no more."

Too bad the adulterous man had fled the scene; he might have received this massive blessing too.

Until "neither do I condemn you" is hardwired into your psyche, "Go and sin no more" will be impossible. I mean deep down inside. Kneaded into your emotions, instincts, and thoughts. There is "no condemnation" for you if you belong to Christ (Romans 8:1). None. Not now. Not ever.

Even when you sin. Again and again and again. Even when you do the same stupid mistake over and over. Even if anything.

Just what part of "no condemnation" do you not understand?

Why are you beating yourself up? Why do you persist in doing penance? Why do you undervalue the saving work of Christ and routinely try to pay for your own dumb sins?

Christ has said, "Neither do I condemn you; go and sin no more." So why are you still groveling on the ground? Why are you wallowing in habits that break your heart and hurt other people?

Why?

Because, in your soul, the theology of grace has not yet displaced the psychology of legalism.

Grace Deficit Disorder owns your instincts. Grace lies at the surface, maybe, but hasn't sunk in.

But it can. And it will. This is your time. Your moment to shake off the shackles of a lifetime—your moment to experience the breakthrough of grace like that sinful woman did so long ago.

And if you think that's just for other people, you're the one who needs a breakthrough. That's the lesson of the Adulterous Woman.

3. The Four Lepers

Grace Deficit Disorder: Now there were four leprous men at the entrance of the gate; and they said to one another, "Why are we sitting here until we die? If we say, 'We will enter the city,' the famine is in the city, and we shall die there. And if we sit here, we die also. Now therefore, come, let us surrender to the army of the Syrians. If they keep us alive, we shall live; and if they kill us, we shall only die." (2 Kings 7:3, 4)

Grace Breakthrough: And when these lepers came to the outskirts of the camp, they went into one tent and ate and drank, and carried from it silver and gold and clothing, and went and hid them; then they came back and entered another tent, and carried some from there also, and went and hid it. Then they said to one another... "This day is a day of good news..." (2 Kings 7:8, 9)

Today called Hansen's disease—and treatable—the ancient world viewed leprosy as a scourge of the gods. Lepers were unclean. They had to wear a mask. Had to cross to the opposite side of the street when they saw you coming. And had to live in exile from the general population.

That explains why our four lepers sat at the entrance of the gate of an ancient city called Samaria. The city was starving to death. The Syrian army had them surrounded. No food or water went in. No waste went out. It's called a *siege.*

This is the perfect picture of the fallen heart before grace breaks through.

The four lepers think through their options. If we stay here, we die of attrition. If we go into the city, we die of starvation. We do have a third option: go toward the enemy camp. Yeah, they may kill us, but what's the difference? There's always a sliver of hope they'll keep us alive.

They shrug what's left of their shoulders, and *at twilight* head toward the enemy camp.

If you find yourself stuck with no good options in sight might I suggest you try heading toward the crucified Savior Jesus? What's the worst that can happen? If you keep doing what you're doing, you'll keep getting what you're getting. If you go backwards, well, that's what got you into your mess in the first place.

Why not move toward that big scary thing on the horizon called *faith*? Why not try faith in Jesus? He just might keep you alive.

Just like he kept the four lepers alive back at the siege. As the sun has set in the west, they arrive at the enemy camp. To their amazement, they find a vast sea of enemy tents, *all empty.*

God scared the enemy soldiers away—all of them— the Bible says, with a mighty noise, *at twilight* (compare

2 Kings 7:5 with 7:7). This is the same time that the lepers struck out for the camp.

Coincidentally.

Or not.

It makes me wonder what God was waiting for.

Mostly, it's faith. He's waiting for faith. When you step out in faith, God reaches down with grace.

God always answers faith with grace. Even if that faith is laced with doubt. Or shaky. Or tentative. Or reluctant. Or powdery small, like a mustard seed (Luke 17:6).

Faith isn't a work. It has no merit. It is intrinsically neither good nor bad. Faith is simply trust in somebody else, and it's the Somebody Else who possesses the merit.

Our lepers had a doubt-filled, scaredy-cat faith. Yet, in tent after tent, these undeserving, unclean, unloved outcasts found food and water, silver and gold, weapons and clothing, and riches to spare.

They didn't buy it, pay for it, build it, earn it, or deserve it.

They just took it by faith. Just like you can take salvation, sanctification, daily bread, and everything you need from the hand of your heavenly father too.

Grace-though-faith wins again.

2. The Exodus Generation

Grace Deficit Disorder: "Is this not the word that we told you in Egypt, saying, 'Let us alone that we may serve the Egyptians?' For it would have been better for us to serve the Egyptians than that we should die in the wilderness." (Exodus 14:12)

Grace Breakthrough: And Moses said to the people, "Do not be afraid. Stand still, and see the salvation of the LORD, which He will accomplish for you today. For the Egyptians whom you see today, you shall see again no more forever." (Exodus 14:13)

What do you say to people who prefer the mindlessness of slavery over the adventure of liberty?

You say, "Get out of the nest, little bird. Fly. Be free."

And you shove them out of the nest, even as they squawk bloody murder.

If you love them, that is.

Which is exactly why God, through Moses, delivered the children of Israel from slavery in Egypt.

In what had to be the worst moment of their up-and-down lives, the Jews now find themselves hemmed in. The armies of Egypt behind them, and the waters of the Red Sea before them.

Like most Grace Deficit Disorder sufferers, they panicked and turned bitter against God. "We knew it, God! You and Moses are just messing with us! You want us dead!"

With Christ, God is not your enemy. He could no more be against you than he could set himself against Christ. You are one with Jesus. Christ is in you. For God to mess with you, he would have to mess with Christ. Unthinkable.

How often we think low thoughts of God, especially in times of trouble! Remember the mother of all the devil's lies: *God is less than he says he is.*

reality, God is immeasurably faithful. He loves you with an everlasting love. He loves you better than you realize. His grace never fails. His mercies are new every morning. God holds you in his heart. He has inscribed you, the Bible says, on the palms of his hands (Isaiah 49:16). You are his cherished possession.

No matter how stuck you are—even if it's your own dumb fault—God says, "Do not be afraid. Stand still, and see the salvation of the Lord."

If he has to slay a giant, he will. If he has to make the sun stand still, he will. If he has to come down personally into your world, and shed his own blood to redeem your soul, he already did. If he has to part a sea he will.

That's your God.

At the heart of every grace breakthrough is your personal re-discovery of your good God. Who is he? What is he like? Grace is a doctrine, but not just a doctrine. It is a force in the universe, but not just a force. Above all else, grace is a quality that emanates from the heart of God as rays emanate from the sun.

To understand grace is to understand God.

To miss grace—to deny it, shrink it, redefine it, ignore it, or contradict it—is to miss the heart of God.

When God set the ancient Jews free from slavery in Egypt, the sheer grace of that moment totally passed them by. Instead, just because of one setback, their little minds ran right back to despicable thoughts about God.

But God still loved them, so he parted the sea, brought them through on dry ground, and swallowed their enemies in the process.

But the grace didn't stop there.

God led them with a pillar of smoke by day and fire by night, fed them with angels' bread called *manna* every single day, ensured their shoes never wore out, granted victory in every single combat, provided water from rocks and meat from flocks—for decades—and *still*, the people doubted him.

Never underestimate the fallen heart's ability to eclipse the sunshine of grace.

The recurring lesson of the Exodus generation is that some grace breakthroughs just don't stick. Especially when it comes to our thoughts about God.

Fear not, however. God will give you as many breakthroughs as you need. He has a gigantic stockpile of them. He will not rest till it dawns deep inside your heart that Calvary's love is eternal, unconditional, boundless, and free. And God will not rest until your triumphant spirit does not depend on circumstances, but on a deep-rooted knowledge of his great love.

1. Paul

Grace Deficit Disorder: Though I also might have confidence in the flesh. If anyone else thinks he may have confidence in the flesh, I more so: circumcised the eighth day, of the stock of Israel, of the tribe of Benjamin, a Hebrew of the Hebrews; concerning the law, a Pharisee; concerning zeal, persecuting the church; concerning the righteousness which is in the law, blameless. (Philippians 3:4-6)

Grace Breakthrough: "Now it happened, as I journeyed and came near Damascus at about noon, suddenly a great light from heaven shone around me.

> And I fell to the ground and heard a voice saying to me, 'Saul, Saul, why are you persecuting Me?'" (Acts 22:6, 7)

> But what things were gain to me, these I have counted loss for Christ. Yet indeed I also count all things loss for the excellence of the knowledge of Christ Jesus my Lord, for whom I have suffered the loss of all things, and count them as rubbish, that I may gain Christ. (Philippians 3:7, 8)

Of all the breakthroughs in Scripture, the Gold Medal has to go to a man named Saul, a.k.a. Paul, a.k.a. the Christian-Slayer. This rising star in the religious constellation breathed "threats and murder against the disciples of the Lord" (Acts 9:1). There was nothing more virtuous, he thought, than to terrorize these infidels who threatened the very heart of Judaism.

Paul was the poster child for legalism. There's no gentle way to break through a self-righteous, legalistic, holier-than-thou callous as thick as his. Some people just have to learn the hard way.

Everything changed for Paul on the road to Damascus. In an epic moment of tough love, God lit him up, blinded him, and knocked him to the ground. As he groveled in self-imposed darkness, God asked him one big question and offered one weird statement.

The question God asked: *Why are you persecuting Me?* This is not to say that God was his victim, or that God felt threatened. In the biblical language, the word *persecuting* can also mean *prosecuting*, like a district attorney.

When your whole life is a lawsuit against the grace of God, it's going to show up in bizarre actions.

You will pester God to pay you for services rendered. You will hound him to punish the lawbreakers you see. You will question his goodness toward the undeserving. You will condemn the world of slackers who don't work as hard as you. You will moan ceaselessly at the poor treatment you receive at his hand. And you will excel above your peers in every arena of life, thus establishing beyond question your right to maximum good stuff from the hand of God—as well as your right to question his integrity when he doesn't pay out.

Legalists find themselves stuck in a lawsuit loop, relentlessly prosecuting God for not living up to twisted moral standards they have set, all the while questioning the fairness of a God who would routinely drop good stuff on the heads of undeserving riff-raff.

So God forced Saul/Paul to consider the sheer vanity of prosecuting his case against heaven.

Then God served up a weird statement: *It is hard for you to kick against the goads.*

The Greek word, *kentron,* could refer to the tip of a spear, the sting of a scorpion or bee, the quill of a porcupine, or to an iron goad to motivate oxen or horses to move along.

It was also used metaphorically to refer to any force that would spur action, or incentivize progress.

All life long, your loving Father in heaven goads you toward grace. He uses experiences. Teachers. Scripture. Trials. Blessings. Books like this one. The sum of your life experiences is a divine conspiracy to hem you into grace. God uses both the good he causes and the bad others cause in and around you to bring you to the end of yourself. He nudges. He pokes. He prods. He goads you along. He proves the lies of artificial happiness. He disintegrates false crutches and foils foolish resistance to grace.

At the end of it all is an encounter in which you say, "Not I, but Christ" (Galatians 2:20).

That's the plan, at least. These are the goads.

To "kick against the goads" is "to offer vain and perilous or ruinous resistance" (Thayer's Lexicon) to the grace incentives God has sprinkled throughout your life. We've all done it. We've all kicked against the goads. We're natural-born mules, stubbornly determined to save ourselves by the sweat of our stupid successes.

Thank God that he never gives up.

A life spent kicking against the goads can be summed up in one word: *hard.* "It is hard for you to kick against the goads."

Wearisome. Tough. Depressing. Deadening. Fake.

Stop it.

Quit kicking.

End the resistance.

Go with the divine flow, because it spills you into a crystal blue ocean of goodness at the end. And in that ocean, you will see a bright reflection of the smiling face of Jesus, whose shed blood and glorious resurrection made every single speck of grace possible.

Let the grace breakthroughs commence.

Prayer

Gracious Lord,

Break through the scar tissue on my heart. Light up the darkness of my soul. Pierce the hardness, and let your grace break through.

I'm too tired to work any more.

I'm too dirty to keep cleaning myself up.

I'm too stuck to get unstuck without your help.

I'm too little and weak to climb the stairway to heaven.

I'm too satisfied, successful, and rich sometimes to even feel my need of you.

So, Lord, take me up by that high and holy elevator of Grace. Let me ride the coattails of my precious Savior all the way to glory.

You have washed away my sin. Now wash away my legalism too. Heal the festering wounds of Grace Deficit Disorder.

And help me rest always and forever in the finished work of Christ, my Savior.

Let the Grace Breakthroughs Commence.

In the mighty name of Jesus, and by his matchless grace I pray,

Amen.

APPENDIX

GOD'S GRACE PROMISES

Gather the riches of God's promises. Nobody can take away from you those texts from the Bible which you have learned by heart. Let God's promises shine upon your problems. –Corrie Ten Boom (Nazi concentration camp survivor)

A S A SQUIRREL STORES UP NUTS, so God's children should store up God's promises. There are thousands of them in the Bible. They are there for every situation you can imagine.

God has made promises for...

When you are tempted, tired, beaten down, and afraid.

When you have opportunities, sickness, financial problems, and loss.

Promises for when you're happy. Promises for when you're sad.

There's not a situation in your life where God does not have a promise to comfort you, to guide you, to strengthen you, and to help you.

The Bible has thousands of promises just waiting for you to claim. They are the tip of the spear for your Grace Breakthrough. They pierce the callous on your self-sufficient soul, opening you to the grace of the moment.

They are God's grace gems sprinkled through Scripture and are more abundant than human needs.

And yet, when you boil it all down, what matters most is not the boatload of promises God has made to you. There's really one mother of all promises in the Bible. It's a big deal, and a key to your Grace Breakthrough.

The Mother of All Promises

God has made one, big, epic promise to one big epic person: God has made one great promise to the Lord Jesus Christ.

That one promise is simple: "I will bless you."

It's a bigger deal than you might think.

God, in effect, said to Christ: "I will enrich you. I will crown you King of kings. I will seat you on the throne of the cosmos. I will exalt your name. I will give you a people. I will make your name great."

God promised, "I will bless YOU and every person attached to you will experience the overflow of that staggeringly beautiful, mind-blowing blessing."

It's not just a promise, it's The Promise.

God made The Promise to One Person, and every other promise in the Bible flows out of this one, like spokes radiating from a wheel's hub.

Here's the best part of all this: *Every time God keeps a promise to you, he is really keeping The Promise he made to Christ.*

You can bank on it.

God could no more break a promise to you than he could break The Promise to Christ. They're all connected. Even in the darkest, stormiest night of your soul, when you claim God's promise, grace will break through, and by that grace, you will prevail.

When I was a kid in church, we sang this beautiful hymn. I hope its lyrics encourage you to stand every day on the promises of God.

> Standing on the promises of Christ my King,
> Through eternal ages let His praises ring,
> Glory in the highest, I will shout and sing,
> Standing on the promises of God.
>
> Standing, standing,
> Standing on the promises of God my Savior;
> Standing, standing,
> I'm standing on the promises of God.
>
> Standing on the promises that cannot fail,
> When the howling storms of doubt and fear assail,
> By the living Word of God I shall prevail,
> Standing on the promises of God.
> (R. Kelso Carter, 1886, public domain)

Here is a small sampling of Bible promises—a basket full of nuts—for the wise follower of God to store up for future trials.

GOD'S PROMISES IN GENERAL

> By which have been given to us exceedingly great and precious promises, that through these you may be partakers of the divine nature, having escaped the corruption that is in the world through lust. 2 Peter 1:4

"Not one thing has failed of all the good things which the LORD your God spoke concerning you. All have come to pass for you; not one word of them has failed." Joshua 23:14

"For the mountains shall depart And the hills be removed, But My kindness shall not depart from you, Nor shall My covenant of peace be removed," Says the LORD, who has mercy on you." Isaiah 54:10

For all the promises of God in Him are Yes, and in Him Amen, to the glory of God through us. 2 Corinthians 1:20

GOD'S POWERFUL WORD

"Your word I have hidden in my heart, That I might not sin against You!" Psalm 119:11

For the word of God is living and powerful, and sharper than any two-edged sword, piercing even to the division of soul and spirit, and of joints and marrow, and is a discerner of the thoughts and intents of the heart. Hebrews 4:12

"Sanctify them by Your truth. Your word is truth." John 17:17

THE MINISTRY OF ANGELS

The angel of the LORD encamps all around those who fear Him, And delivers them. Psalm 34:7

Are they not all ministering spirits sent forth to minister for those who will inherit salvation? Hebrews 1:14

For He shall give His angels charge over you, To keep you in all your ways. In their hands they shall bear you up, Lest you dash your foot against a stone. Psalm 91:11, 12

OUR STATUS AS PRIESTS AND KINGS

And has made us kings and priests to His God and Father, to Him be glory and dominion forever and ever. Amen." Revelation 1:6

"But you are a chosen generation, a royal priesthood, a holy nation, His own special people, that you may proclaim the praises of Him who called you out of darkness into His marvelous light." 1 Peter 2:9

HELP IN TROUBLES

Your righteousness is like the great mountains; Your judgments are a great deep; O LORD, You preserve man and beast. How precious is Your lovingkindness, O God! Therefore the children of men put their trust under the shadow of Your wings. Psalm 36:6, 7

No evil shall befall you, Nor shall any plague come near your dwelling. Psalm 91:10

For His anger is but for a moment, His favor is for life; Weeping may endure for a night, But joy comes in the morning. Psalm 30:5

Many are the afflictions of the righteous, But the LORD delivers him out of them all. Psalm 34:19

Why are you cast down, O my soul? And why are you disquieted within me? Hope in God; For I shall yet praise Him, The help of my countenance and my God. Psalm 42:11

The LORD opens the eyes of the blind; The LORD raises those who are bowed down; The LORD loves the righteous. Psalm 146:8

Those who sow in tears Shall reap in joy. He who continually goes forth weeping, Bearing seed for sowing, Shall doubtless come again with rejoicing, Bringing his sheaves with him. Psalm 126:5, 6

For I know the thoughts that I think toward you, says the LORD, thoughts of peace and not of evil, to give you a future and a hope. Jeremiah 29:11

Therefore they shall come and sing in the height of Zion, Streaming to the goodness of the LORD—For wheat and new wine and oil, For the young of the flock and the herd; Their souls shall be like a well-watered garden, And they shall sorrow no more at all. Then shall the virgin rejoice in the dance, And the young men and the old, together; For I will turn their mourning to joy, Will comfort them, And make them rejoice rather than sorrow. Jeremiah 31:12, 13

Come, and let us return to the LORD; For He has torn, but He will heal us; He has stricken, but He will bind us up. Hosea 6:1

SUPPORT IN TROUBLE

The LORD also will be a refuge for the oppressed, A refuge in times of trouble. Psalm 9:9

Wait on the LORD; Be of good courage, And He shall strengthen your heart; Wait, I say, on the LORD! Psalm 27:14

When my father and my mother forsake me, Then the LORD will take care of me. Psalm 27:10

Though he fall, he shall not be utterly cast down; For the LORD upholds him with His hand." "But the salvation of the righteous is from the LORD; He is their strength in the time of trouble. Psalm 37:24, 39

The LORD is my rock and my fortress and my deliverer; My God, my strength, in whom I will trust; My shield and the horn of my salvation, my stronghold. Psalm 18:2

God is our refuge and strength, A very present help in trouble. Therefore we will not fear, Even though the earth be removed, And though the mountains be carried into the midst of the sea; Though its waters roar and be troubled, Though the mountains shake with its swelling. Selah. Psalm 46:1-3

Cast your burden on the LORD, And He shall sustain you; He shall never permit the righteous to be moved. Psalm 55:22

Blessed is he who considers the poor; The LORD will deliver him in time of trouble. Psalm 41:1

My flesh and my heart fail; But God is the strength of my heart and my portion forever. Psalm 73:26

For the Lord will not cast off forever. Though He causes grief, Yet He will show compassion According to the multitude of His mercies. For He does not afflict willingly, Nor grieve the children of men. Lamentations 3:31-33

O LORD, my strength and my fortress, My refuge in the day of affliction... Jeremiah 16:19

We are hard pressed on every side, yet not crushed; we are perplexed, but not in despair; persecuted, but not forsaken; struck down, but not destroyed. 2 Corinthians 4:8, 9

FOR GOD'S VENGEANCE & VICTORY

Though I walk in the midst of trouble, You will revive me; You will stretch out Your hand Against the wrath of my enemies, And Your right hand will save me. Psalm 138:7

For the LORD your God is He who goes with you, to fight for you against your enemies, to save you. Deuteronomy 20:4

Through God we will do valiantly, For it is He who shall tread down our enemies. Psalm 60:12

Now look, God Himself is with us as our head... 2 Chronicles 13:12

Behold, all those who were incensed against you Shall be ashamed and disgraced; They shall be as nothing, And those who strive with you shall perish. You shall seek them and not find them-- Those who contended with you. Those who war against you Shall be as nothing, As a nonexistent thing. Isaiah 41:11, 12

"But I will deliver you in that day," says the LORD, "and you shall not be given into the hand of the men of whom you are afraid. "For I will surely deliver you, and you shall not fall by the sword; but your life shall be as a prize to you, because you have put your trust in Me," says the LORD." Jeremiah 39:17, 18

So he answered, "Do not fear, for those who are with us are more than those who are with them." 2 Kings 6:16

And Asa cried out to the LORD his God, and said, "LORD, it is nothing for You to help, whether with many or with those who have no power; help us, O LORD our God, for we rest on You, and in Your name we go against this multitude. O LORD, You are our God; do not let man prevail against You!" 2 Chronicles 14:11

Show Your marvelous lovingkindness by Your right hand, O You who save those who trust in You From those who rise up against them. Psalm 17:7

For in the time of trouble He shall hide me in His pavilion; In the secret place of His tabernacle He shall hide me; He shall set me high upon a rock. And now my head shall be lifted up above my enemies all around me; Therefore I will offer sacrifices of joy in His tabernacle; I will sing, yes, I will sing praises to the LORD. Psalm 27:5, 6

The wicked watches the righteous, And seeks to slay him. The LORD will not leave him in his hand, Nor condemn him when he is judged. And the LORD shall help them and deliver them; He shall deliver them from the wicked, And save them, Because they trust in Him. Psalm 37:32, 33, 40

His heart is established; He will not be afraid, Until he sees his desire upon his enemies. Psalm 112:8

When a man's ways please the LORD, He makes even his enemies to be at peace with him. Proverbs 16:7

"Indeed they shall surely assemble, but not because of Me. Whoever assembles against you shall fall for your sake. No weapon formed against you shall prosper, And every tongue which rises against you in judgment You shall condemn. This is the heritage of the servants of the LORD, And their righteousness is from Me," Says the LORD." Isaiah 54:15, 17

"And shall God not avenge His own elect who cry out day and night to Him, though He bears long with them? I tell you that He will avenge them speedily. Nevertheless, when the Son of Man comes, will He really find faith on the earth?" Luke 18:7, 8

So we may boldly say: "The LORD is my helper; I will not fear. What can man do to me?" Hebrews 13:6

That we should be saved from our enemies And from the hand of all who hate us, To grant us that we, Being delivered from the hand of our enemies, Might serve Him without fear, In holiness and righteousness before Him all the days of our life. Luke 1:71, 74, 75

PROMISES FOR SICKNESS & OLD AGE

So you shall serve the LORD your God, and He will bless your bread and your water. And I will take sickness away from the midst of you. Exodus 23:25

"If you diligently heed the voice of the LORD your God and do what is right in His sight, give ear to His commandments and keep all His statutes, I will put none of the diseases on you which I have brought on the Egyptians. For I am the LORD who heals you." Exodus 15:26

Surely He shall deliver you from the snare of the fowler And from the perilous pestilence. You shall not be afraid of the terror by night, Nor of the arrow that flies by day, Nor of the pestilence that walks in darkness, Nor of the destruction that lays waste at noonday. Psalm 91:3, 5, 6

"Who forgives all your iniquities, Who heals all your diseases," Psalm 103:3

Do not cast me off in the time of old age; Do not forsake me when my strength fails. Psalm 71:9

Even to your old age, I am He, And even to gray hairs I will carry you! I have made, and I will bear; Even I will carry, and will deliver you. Isaiah 46:4

The silver-haired head is a crown of glory, If it is found in the way of righteousness. Proverbs 16:31

IN TIMES OF FINANCIAL STRESS

Who executes justice for the oppressed, Who gives food to the hungry. The LORD gives freedom to the prisoners. Psalm 146:7

I will deliver you from all your uncleannesses. I will call for the grain and multiply it, and bring no famine upon you. And I will multiply the fruit of your trees and the increase of your fields, so that you need never again bear the reproach of famine among the nations. Ezekiel 36:29, 30

Ask the LORD for rain In the time of the latter rain. The LORD will make flashing clouds; He will give them showers of rain, Grass in the field for everyone. Zechariah 10:1

Though the fig tree may not blossom, Nor fruit be on the vines; Though the labor of the olive may fail, And the fields yield no food; Though the flock may be cut

off from the fold, And there be no herd in the stalls--
Yet I will rejoice in the LORD, I will joy in the God of
my salvation. Habakkuk 3:17, 18

But He answered and said, "It is written, 'Man shall
not live by bread alone, but by every word that
proceeds from the mouth of God." Matthew 4:4

FROM WITCHCRAFT

For there is no sorcery against Jacob, Nor any
divination against Israel. Numbers 23:23

ABSENT/FAILED/IMPERFECT PARENTS

He administers justice for the fatherless and the
widow, and loves the stranger, giving him food and
clothing. Deuteronomy 10:18

But You have seen, for You observe trouble and grief,
To repay it by Your hand. The helpless commits
himself to You; You are the helper of the fatherless.
To do justice to the fatherless and the oppressed,
That the man of the earth may oppress no more.
Psalm 10:14, 18

IN TIME OF DEATH

Our God is the God of salvation; And to God the Lord
belong escapes from death. Psalm 68:20

Precious in the sight of the LORD Is the death of His
saints. Psalm 116:15

Have mercy on me, O LORD! Consider my trouble from
those who hate me, You who lift me up from the gates
of death. Psalm 9:13

GOD'S MERCY

All the paths of the LORD are mercy and truth, To such
as keep His covenant and His testimonies. The secret
of the LORD is with those who fear Him, And He will
show them His covenant. Psalm 25:10, 14

Blessed be the God and Father of our Lord Jesus Christ, who has blessed us with every spiritual blessing in the heavenly places in Christ, just as He chose us in Him before the foundation of the world, that we should be holy and without blame before Him in love... In Him we have redemption through His blood, the forgiveness of sins, according to the riches of His grace which He made to abound toward us in all wisdom and prudence. Ephesians 1:3, 4, 7, 8

As His divine power has given to us all things that pertain to life and godliness, through the knowledge of Him who called us by glory and virtue, by which have been given to us exceedingly great and precious promises, that through these you may be partakers of the divine nature, having escaped the corruption that is in the world through lust. 2 Peter 1:3, 4

Moreover whom He predestined, these He also called; whom He called, these He also justified; and whom He justified, these He also glorified. Romans 8:30

SALVATION

In the LORD all the descendants of Israel Shall be justified, and shall glory. Isaiah 45:25

Being justified freely by His grace through the redemption that is in Christ Jesus. Romans 3:24

There is therefore now no condemnation to those who are in Christ Jesus, who do not walk according to the flesh, but according to the Spirit. Who shall bring a charge against God's elect? It is God who justifies. Who is he who condemns? It is Christ who died, and furthermore is also risen, who is even at the right hand of God, who also makes intercession for us. Romans 8:1, 33, 34

I have blotted out, like a thick cloud, your transgressions, And like a cloud, your sins. Return to Me, for I have redeemed you. Isaiah 44:22

He will not always strive with us, Nor will He keep His anger forever. He has not dealt with us according to our sins, Nor punished us according to our iniquities. For as the heavens are high above the earth, So great is His mercy toward those who fear Him; As far as the east is from the west, So far has He removed our transgressions from us. Psalm 103:9-12

Who is a God like You, Pardoning iniquity And passing over the transgression of the remnant of His heritage? He does not retain His anger forever, Because He delights in mercy. He will again have compassion on us, And will subdue our iniquities. You will cast all our sins Into the depths of the sea. Micah 7:18, 19

"Come now, and let us reason together," Says the LORD, "Though your sins are like scarlet, They shall be as white as snow; Though they are red like crimson, They shall be as wool." Isaiah 1:18

I will cleanse them from all their iniquity by which they have sinned against Me, and I will pardon all their iniquities by which they have sinned and by which they have transgressed against Me. Jeremiah 33:8

If we confess our sins, He is faithful and just to forgive us our sins and to cleanse us from all unrighteousness. 1 John 1:9

BACKSLIDING

Go and proclaim these words toward the north, and say: "Return, backsliding Israel," says the LORD; "I will not cause My anger to fall on you. For I am merciful," says the LORD; "I will not remain angry forever. Return, you backsliding children, And I will heal your backslidings." Indeed we do come to You, For You are the LORD our God. Jeremiah 3:12, 22

I will heal their backsliding, I will love them freely, For My anger has turned away from him. Hosea 14:4

JESUS CHRIST

And she will bring forth a Son, and you shall call His name JESUS, for He will save His people from their sins. Matthew 1:21

In Him we have redemption through His blood, the forgiveness of sins, according to the riches of His grace Ephesians 1:7

This is a faithful saying and worthy of all acceptance, that Christ Jesus came into the world to save sinners, of whom I am chief. 1 Timothy 1:15

The next day John saw Jesus coming toward him, and said, "Behold! The Lamb of God who takes away the sin of the world!" John 1:29

My little children, these things I write to you, so that you may not sin. And if anyone sins, we have an Advocate with the Father, Jesus Christ the righteous. And He Himself is the propitiation for our sins, and not for ours only but also for the whole world. I write to you, little children, Because your sins are forgiven you for His name's sake. 1 John 2:1, 2, 12

TEMPTATION

Yet in all these things we are more than conquerors through Him who loved us. Romans 8:37

No temptation has overtaken you except such as is common to man; but God is faithful, who will not allow you to be tempted beyond what you are able, but with the temptation will also make the way of escape, that you may be able to bear it. 1 Corinthians 10:13

Then the Lord knows how to deliver the godly out of temptations and to reserve the unjust under punishment for the day of judgment. 2 Peter 2:9

You are of God, little children, and have overcome them, because He who is in you is greater than he who is in the world. 1 John 4:4

HOLY SPIRIT

Jesus answered and said to her, "If you knew the gift of God, and who it is who says to you, 'Give Me a drink,' you would have asked Him, and He would have given you living water.... But whoever drinks of the water that I shall give him will never thirst. But the water that I shall give him will become in him a fountain of water springing up into everlasting life." John 4:10, 14

That good thing which was committed to you, keep by the Holy Spirit who dwells in us. 2 Timothy 1:14

But you shall receive power when the Holy Spirit has come upon you; and you shall be witnesses to Me in Jerusalem, and in all Judea and Samaria, and to the end of the earth. Acts 1:8

So he answered and said to me: "This *is* the word of the LORD to Zerubbabel: 'Not by might nor by power, but by My Spirit,' Says the LORD of hosts." Zechariah 4:6

And do not be drunk with wine, in which is dissipation; but be filled with the Spirit. Ephesians 5:18

In Him you also *trusted*, after you heard the word of truth, the gospel of your salvation; in whom also, having believed, you were sealed with the Holy Spirit of promise. Ephesians 1:13

Now hope does not disappoint, because the love of God has been poured out in our hearts by the Holy Spirit who was given to us. Romans 5:5

Now He who establishes us with you in Christ and has anointed us *is* God, who also has sealed us and given us the Spirit in our hearts as a guarantee. 2 Corinthians 1:21, 22

GOD'S FAITHFULNESS

Therefore know that the LORD your God, He is God, the faithful God who keeps covenant and mercy for a thousand generations with those who love Him and keep His commandments. Deuteronomy 7:9

God is not a man, that He should lie, Nor a son of man, that He should repent. Has He said, and will He not do? Or has He spoken, and will He not make it good? Numbers 23:19

Through the LORD'S mercies we are not consumed, Because His compassions fail not. They are new every morning; Great is Your faithfulness. "The LORD is my portion," says my soul, "Therefore I hope in Him!" The LORD is good to those who wait for Him, To the soul who seeks Him. It is good that one should hope and wait quietly For the salvation of the LORD. Lamentations 3:22-26

Keep in Touch

Website: www.maxgrace.com
Twitter: www.twitter.com/BillGiovannetti
Facebook: www.facebook.com/PastorBillG

Please look for all the books in the *GRACE RESET* series:
Grace Intervention
*Grace Rehab**
*Grace Breakthrough**
*Grace Renovation (2017)**

(*Companion Study Guide Available)